Everyday Korean

ALSO BY KIM SUNÉE
Trail of Crumbs: Hunger, Love, and the Search for Home
A Mouthful of Stars: A Constellation of Favorite Recipes from My World Travels

ALSO BY LEELA CYD
Food with Friends: The Art of Simple Gatherings

연두부

오이김치

아기무우김치

Everyday Korean

FRESH, MODERN RECIPES FOR HOME COOKS

Kim Sunée and Seung Hee Lee

PHOTOGRAPHY BY LEELA CYD

The Countryman Press
A division of W. W. Norton & Company
Independent Publishers Since 1923

For information about permission to reproduce selections from this book,
write to Permissions, The Countryman Press, 500 Fifth Avenue, New York, NY 10110

For information about special discounts for bulk purchases, please contact
W. W. Norton Special Sales at specialsales@wwnorton.com or 800-233-4830

Manufacturing through Imago
Book design by Nick Caruso Design
Production manager: Devon Zahn

The Countryman Press
www.countrymanpress.com

A division of W. W. Norton & Company, Inc.
500 Fifth Avenue, New York, NY 10110
www.wwnorton.com

978-1-68268-114-5

10 9 8 7 6 5 4 3 2 1

Contents

Preface

If Japanese food was
a romantic comedy,
Korean food would be
an action movie.

—Chef Hooni Kim

Welcome to the *Everyday Korean* kitchen. Whether you're a cook just starting out or a well-seasoned chef, we hope that you are as excited about cooking with Korean flavors as we are to share these recipes with you. Creating this book has truly been a labor of love, a collaboration between two food-obsessed enthusiastic cooks. If we're not shopping, cooking, and eating, we are planning the next dish, the next meal, the next way to share the table with those we love.

We met in Seoul in 2008; Seung Hee was my interpreter during the book tour for the Korean-language edition of my memoir, *Trail of Crumbs: Hunger, Love, and the Search for Home.* After an emotional journey through Seoul (revisiting orphanages and markets in hopes that I might find some trace of my birth family) and many shared meals, not to mention glasses of bubbles and *soju,* we bonded over our love of food, Seung Hee acting as the culinary guide, helping me taste my way through my birth country and feel at home.

Seung Hee, who would soon leave to study at Johns Hopkins, also trained at the prestigious Taste of Korea Institute, a research organization dedicated to the preservation of Korean royal court cuisine, Korean culinary traditions, and reviving traditional recipes for modern-day kitchens.

Thanks to her, we were allowed access one day during the filming of a KBS documentary filmed by Hongseok "Roy" Ro.

We steamed rice cakes wrapped in ramie—fragrant leaves of the nettle family—and braised short ribs to be served with perfect diamond-shape egg garnishes. I was admonished repeatedly for not perfectly slicing the raw chestnuts and fresh jujube into equal-size julienne pieces. Despite my inadequacies, I was happy in that kitchen. We were a group of women working together to re-create flavors from dishes deeply rooted in tradition and history.

I've often been asked about taste memory and what it means, especially for a cuisine that I didn't grow up eating; I was in a kitchen thousands of miles away, watching my adoptive grandfather stir huge pots of crawfish bisque and red beans and rice and fry up *panéed* veal to top with lump crabmeat or a deep red gravy. Later, throughout the ten years I lived in France and traveled throughout Europe, I'd come to taste and cook freshly unearthed truffles and all manner of foie gras as well as the rustic foods of Provence, including *soupe d'épautre*, garlic-laden *pistou*, and caramelized onion *pissaladière*.

As much as I was fascinated by Korean cuisine, I was also intimidated by the idea of actually cooking with techniques and ingredients so different from my culinary background. But I've always felt deeply connected to the flavors and beauty of this rustic hearty cuisine.

Over the years, we've talked about writing this book together with a focus in re-creating delicious interpretations of Korean dishes with deep flavor and ease of preparation using ingredients familiar to the non-Korean home cook. Many of the recipes are based on traditional Korean recipes, many from Seung Hee's family, but with a modern twist using fresh, seasonal ingredients. Others are reinterpretations with new flavors influenced by our respective travels and what we like to cook and eat on a daily basis.

I've learned so much about the food of my birth country in the process. I hope that this culinary journey will inspire you as well to include traditional Korean flavors in your daily cooking repertoire. And while I have yet to find my birth family, I did find a sister for life and a place at the Korean Table. And for that, I will always be grateful.

Kim Sunée, 2017

As a child, I ate everything from mountain greens to frog legs. My grandmother, who was my caregiver when my mother was at work, never left the kitchen. Naturally, that's where I hung out. She was a culinary wizard and together we foraged dandelion greens to make kimchi, dried acorns on the balcony for acorn jelly, and much more. The kitchen was my playground.

My mother, despite her demanding full-time job as a professor, always put homemade food on the table. That was her mantra—good nourishment for a healthy body. As the firstborn daughter, I was my mom's best helper. She would call me from work at five p.m. to wash the rice, and remind me again in thirty minutes to press the rice cooker. By the time she got home, the freshly cooked rice was ready for all of us.

My love for food has an adventurous side, thanks to my father who grew up in Busan—the largest port city in Korea. One of the many food stories in our family is of a three-year-old me eating a live octopus on a stick, like a lollipop. My father and I would go out in the ocean for sea urchin, and he would crack them right out of the water and put the lobes of delicious *uni* in my mouth.

Many years later, when I had to pick a major in college, I went with food and nutrition. If I couldn't go to a culinary school, I thought that was the next best thing. My wise mentor advised me, if I were to study abroad, I needed to know real Korean food beyond Korean BBQ that most foreigners are familiar with. That's when I started attending the Taste of Korea Institute on weekends—where royal recipes are modified for the modern kitchen all while honoring tradition. That's when I gained respect for every ingredient, and the wisdom of all those before me on how foods should be prepared and preserved. For example, soy sauce was always kept outdoors in *onggi*, earthenware made with Korean clay that's porous and keeps the sauce alive. When new batches of soy sauce are made, they go into a large *onggi*, and subsequently smaller *onggi* lined up like Russian dolls; any leftover soy is poured into the *onggi* from the previous year, all the way down to a fifteen-year-old aged soy sauce. My life changed forever when I first tasted fifteen-year-old soy sauce. It was dense like caramel. And to season 10 pounds of meat, I needed only 1 tablespoon of that concentrated concoction. That's when I truly understood what my mentor wanted me to experience—the true beauty of Korean cuisine—and to share this beauty with people outside of Korea.

And then I met Sunée, as her interpreter in 2008 in Seoul, just before getting ready to head to Johns Hopkins to start a public health PhD. I was an insecure twenty-five-year-old who was busy pretending to be someone I thought I should be. I'll never forget our meal at OK Kitchen in Itaewon—it was the first time I had tasted duck pastrami, *brandade*, *bottarga* pasta, and *budino*. All flavors familiar to Sunée, who had eaten and lived in France for ten years. But for me, I realized that "Western" food is so much more than pizza and hamburgers. We kept in touch over the years and always had the idea of writing this cookbook together with recipes that made me who I am today, such as Grandma's Pumpkin Soup and Traditional Napa Cabbage Kimchi. But most of the recipes are ones I learned to modify over the last eight years cooking in an American kitchen.

Our goal here isn't to be "authentic" but, rather, to be inclusive, incorporating flavors that make sense in our everyday eating. To me, food memories are worth more than jewels. This book contains recipes that have a special place in my heart. I hope you make incredible food memories cooking with our book.

Seung Hee Lee, 2017

Introduction

How Best to Use This Book?

If these flavors and ingredients are new to you, we encourage you to first read through the section "The Korean Pantry and Other Key Ingredients" and the glossary. This will help you stock up properly to get you started on your Korean cooking adventure. We've also offered substitutions and sometimes shortcut versions when it makes sense. Many of these ingredients are available in the Asian section of larger supermarkets, and if they are not there, seek out a good Asian market in your town. There's always online shopping, too. H Mart will deliver most nonrefrigerated items and in some states will deliver fresh items as well. Also try Koamart.com, Hangyangmart.com and for the United Kingdom and the rest of Europe, sous-chef.co.uk. And for cookware, ekitchenary.com.

As with any new recipe, it's best to read through the entire recipe before getting started. Your cooking life will be so much easier if you measure and prep the ingredients as much as possible before you start; it's always easier to know where you're going than having to backtrack. The more you become familiar with the *Everyday Korean* flavors, the more you'll feel comfortable cooking these recipes on a regular basis and find that many of the dishes are meant to be shared. More than anything, we hope you enjoy your time in the kitchen and at the table.

The Korean Table

If you've been to a Korean restaurant or have been invited to share a meal in a Korean home, you're probably familiar with the tabletop BBQ (in restaurants) as well as the endless array of small side dishes and condiments known as *banchan*; *ban* ("a bowl of rice") and *chan* ("something extra") are the essential components of a Korean meal, so much so that a common greeting in Korean for "How are you?" is "Have you eaten (a bowl of) rice?"

Soy Sauce

Garlic

Pine Nuts

Jujube

Gochujang

Toasted Seaweed

Dried Anchovies (Small)

Sesame Oil

Miso

Rice Vinegar

Dried Shiitake

Doenjang (Soy Paste)

KEWPIE
MAYONNAISE

500g

Dried Kelp

Oyster Sauce

Black Sesame Seeds

Gochugaru
(Korean Chili Flakes)

Short Grain Rice

Dried Persimmon

Toasted Sesame Seeds

Ginger

Dried Anchovies (Large)

Cinnamon

Mung Beans

Korean Sea Salt

Honey

Bansang, the basic table or meal (*sang* meaning "table") consists of rice (*bap*), soup (*guk* or *tang*), sauce (*gochujang* or soy sauce), a stew or casserole (*jjigae*), and kimchi. The number of *banchan* served varies and historically reflected the affluence of those at the table; less affluent people or "commoners" would eat three to five additional *banchan* to make a three- or five-*cheop bansang*, while the nobles would eat nine additional *banchan*. The table setting for the king is called *surasang*: *sura* referring to "king's rice," and the *sang* (table) to the king's meal, which includes up to thirty-four different kinds of *banchan* or side dishes.

The Korean Pantry and Other Key Ingredients

Here is a list of some basic ingredients to get you started on your Korean cooking adventure. For more on these and other ingredients not listed below, please see the glossary (page 243).

Asian pear/Korean pear
Cabbage
Cucumber
Doenjang
Dried anchovies *(myeolchi)*
Dumpling wrappers
Eggs
Fish sauce
Garlic
Ginger
Gochugaru
Gochujang
Green onions
Kelp *(dashima)*
Kimchi
Noodles
Perilla
Radish
Rice
Rice cakes *(ddeok)*
Rice flour
Rice vinegar or cider vinegar
Seaweed
Sesame oil
Sesame seeds, white and black
Salted shrimp *(saeu-jeot)*
Soju
Soy sauce

Chapter 1.

Essential Sauces and Condiments

GOCHUJANG VINAIGRETTE

Cho-gochujang

This tangy vinegar-spiked condiment is the Korean equivalent to ketchup; Koreans love it with everything! It's a great complement to sashimi and our rice bowl recipes (Rice Bowl with Assorted Vegetable Banchan, page 150; Sashimi Rice Bowl, page 149; and Korean-Style Poké, page 147). Add some to your favorite BBQ sauce, brush on grilled chicken, stir into a traditional vinaigrette, use as a vegetable dipping sauce, drizzle over eggs, or stir into hummus for a gentle kick. It's also delicious mixed with a little mayo for dipping hot crisp French fries. **MAKES ABOUT 1 ½ CUPS**

½ cup *gochujang*

½ cup rice vinegar or cider vinegar

1½ tablespoons fresh lemon juice

¼ cup granulated sugar

1 tablespoon minced garlic

1 tablespoon minced green onion

1 tablespoon toasted sesame seeds,
plus more for garnish

Place all the ingredients in a small bowl; stir well to combine, incorporating the *gochujang* by pressing with the back of a spoon against the side of the bowl. The consistency should be similar to that of a thick syrup. Can be stored, in an airtight container, in the refrigerator for up to 2 weeks. *Gochujang* absorbs liquid, so it may thicken over time; simply stir in some warm water or fresh lemon juice to loosen it up.

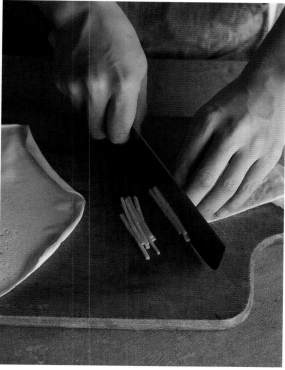

Chapter 2

Getting Started
Pancakes, Fritters, and Small Bites

It's said that Koreans crave *jeon* (pancakes) when it's raining; the sizzling sound when the batter hits the hot pan mimics the music of rain drops. They are typically served with Soy-Vinegar Dipping Sauce (page 21), but if you want a spicy kick, serve with Gochujang Vinaigrette (page 18) as well.

SPICY KALE AND BACON
GOCHUJANG PANCAKES

Jangddeok

Jangddeok are savory pancakes sassed up with luscious *gochujang* paste folded into the batter. We use bacon in place of ground pork; aside from the fact that it makes almost everything delicious, bacon is sometimes easier to have on hand than the traditional fresh ground pork. As to the batter consistency, think more of a fritter batter, chunky with ingredients and a barely there binder. As the kale cooks down, it will become more of a flat, crispy pancake.

MAKES 4 OR 5 PANCAKES

2 cups warm water

2 tablespoons *gochujang*

4 cups packed thinly sliced kale, stems removed (about 1 bunch)

4 green onions, cut into thirds and thinly sliced

2 cups all-purpose flour

4 strips thick-cut bacon, chopped

2 large eggs

4 tablespoons neutral oil, such as canola or grapeseed

FOR SERVING Soy-Vinegar Dipping Sauce (page 21)

Combine the water and *gochujang* in a small bowl, stirring with a large spoon and pressing the paste against the side of the bowl to loosen it up.

Place the kale, green onions, flour, bacon, eggs, and *gochujang* mixture in a large bowl. Mix gently just to combine, preferably using your hands to carefully incorporate the ingredients. The batter should appear as if the flour is barely binding the vegetables and bacon together. Not to worry, though; it will all come together in the pan. As the kale cooks, the liquid that's released will also help bind the batter.

Heat about 1½ tablespoons of the oil in a heavy-bottomed skillet over medium-high heat. Test the skillet by adding a tiny splash of water or a bit of the batter; the oil and batter should dance and crack and sizzle. When the oil is hot, add the mixture to the pan, using a ladle or a ¾-cup measuring cup, and press down gently, using the back of a spatula, to even out the mixture into a pancake. Cook until golden and crispy, about 3 minutes. If the pancake is steaming and not sizzling, increase the heat and add another drop or two of oil. Gently flip and cook the other side for another minute or two until golden; try not to flip more than once. Repeat with the remaining oil and batter. Place the pancakes on a wire cooling rack to prevent steaming; rewarm in the skillet, if needed, to crisp up the edges before cutting into wedges and serving. Serve warm with Soy-Vinegar Dipping Sauce. If making ahead, reheat a minute or two in a dry skillet.

CRISPY MUNG BEAN PANCAKES

Bindaetteok or Nokdu Jeon

These lovely *jeon* feature the mung bean (a.k.a. *moong dal*), which grows into the ubiquitous fresh bean sprout, quintessential to Asian cooking. Dried mung beans are often found in Indian cooking. Here we use dried yellow mung beans that are soaked, then pureed, so no added binder is necessary. Make sure to buy dried yellow mung beans; dried green mung beans need to be peeled.

If modifying the recipe, be sure to use equal parts beans to water as they get pureed together.

These crisp up beautifully in the skillet and are best served hot, but leftovers can be warmed in a dry skillet. Try topped with avocado slices or a poached egg for a quick protein-packed breakfast or snack. **MAKES 4 TO 6 SERVINGS**

1½ cups dried yellow mung beans

1½ cups water

½ cup diced bacon or ground pork (optional)

1 cup fresh bean sprouts

2 green onions, thinly sliced

1 jalapeño pepper, thinly sliced

3 to 4 tablespoons neutral oil, such as canola or grapeseed, for frying

FOR SERVING Soy-Vinegar Dipping Sauce (page 21)

Place the dried mung beans in a colander and rinse well, then place in a bowl and add 1½ cups of water. Let soak for at least 1 hour and up to overnight (the longer they soak, the softer the texture). Place the beans along with their soaking liquid in a food processor or blender; pulse into a smooth puree. Transfer the mixture back to its bowl. Add the bacon, if using, and the mung bean sprouts, green onion, and jalapeño; stir to combine.

Heat about 1½ tablespoons of the oil in a heavy-bottomed skillet over medium-high heat. Test the skillet by adding a splash of water or a bit of the batter; the oil and batter should dance and crack and sizzle. When the oil is hot, add the mixture to the pan, using a ladle or a ¾-cup measuring cup, and press down gently, using the back of a spatula, to even out the mixture into a pancake. Cook until golden, about 3 minutes. If the pancake is steaming and not sizzling, increase the heat and add another drop of oil. Gently flip and cook the other side until golden; try not to flip more than once. Repeat with the remaining oil and batter. Place the pancakes on a wire cooling rack; rewarm in the skillet, if needed, to crisp up the edges before cutting into wedges and serving. Serve warm with Soy-Vinegar Dipping Sauce. Reheat any leftovers in a dry skillet.

NOTE: Using mung beans—a low glycemic index food—in place of flour is a satisfying way to enjoy delicious savory pancakes without worrying about gluten or an insulin surge.

GREEN ONION AND SEAFOOD PANCAKES

Haemul Pajeon

This is a quick and delicious appetizer or snack for any time. We highly recommend using a heavy-bottomed pan, such as a well-seasoned cast-iron skillet. Even though the green onion pancake is perhaps the most well-known of all the *jeon*, you can make these with leftover ingredients from making kimchi, which usually includes equal parts green onion, Korean chive, and *minari*. Our favorite is to stud the pancakes while in the skillet with fresh oysters or shrimp. Traditionally these are served with Soy-Vinegar Dipping Sauce, but are equally delicious with Gochujang Vinaigrette.

MAKES 4 SERVINGS AS AN APPETIZER

3 cups loosely packed green onions, or combination of green onions and chives

1 cup plus 1 tablespoon all-purpose flour

1 cup water

1 large egg

1 teaspoon fish sauce, or ½ teaspoon fine sea salt

Neutral oil, such as canola or grapeseed, duck fat, or beef tallow, for panfrying

1 pint fresh raw oysters, drained, or fresh raw shrimp or bay scallops (optional)

1 to 2 red or green chiles, cut into thin slices (optional)

FOR SERVING Soy-Vinegar Dipping Sauce (page 21) or Gochujang Vinaigrette (page 18)

Wash, trim, and pat dry the green onions. Cut into 2-inch-long pieces and then into thin matchsticks; place in a large bowl. Add the flour, water, egg, and fish sauce. Mix gently just to combine, preferably using your hands to carefully incorporate the ingredients and to not overwork the batter.

Heat about 1½ tablespoons of the oil in a heavy-bottomed skillet over medium-high heat; the oil should dance and sizzle. Scoop one-half of the batter into the very hot skillet and press down with the back of a spoon or spatula to make an even pancake. If the pancake is steaming and not sizzling, increase the heat and add another drop of oil. If adding seafood and chiles, lightly dust them with flour (as they'll adhere better to the pancake) and then stud the pancake with them. When the bottom turns golden brown, about 4 minutes, flip and press gently with the spatula. Lower or increase the heat depending on whether they are browning too quickly or not sizzling enough. Cook for another 3 to 4 minutes, until crispy around the edges and golden all over. Transfer to a wire cooling rack or wooden cutting board and let cool slightly. Slice with a knife or kitchen shears into wedges before serving. Serve with Soy-Vinegar Dipping Sauce or Gochujang Vinaigrette. Reheat any leftovers in a dry skillet.

POTATO PANCAKES

Gamja Jeon

In Kangwon province, in the far northeast of South Korea, where the terrain is mostly mountainous with very limited land for farming, potatoes are the main staple. And potato pancakes and potato *tteok* (made with potato starch and stuffed with kidney bean paste), can be found at almost every rest stop and at corner markets.

Think of these as Korean latkes. We use the starch from the potatoes as a binder, so no extra flour or eggs are needed. The result is a chewy, almost translucent pancake. For this recipe, skip fancy potatoes and stick to a starchy variety, such as russet. Keep in mind that the finer the grate, the more starch you'll be able to extract, which will reward you with a soft, silky center. If you're in a hurry, you can squeeze the liquid out of the potato and add 1 tablespoon of dry potato starch. **MAKES 4 SERVINGS**

1 pound potatoes, preferably russet or other starchy variety

About 2 cups water

½ teaspoon fine sea salt

3 tablespoons neutral oil, such as canola or grapeseed

FOR SERVING Soy-Vinegar Dipping Sauce (page 21) or Everyday Korean All-Purpose Sauce (page 25)

Peel the potatoes and grate, using a cheese grater (see headnote). Place the grated potatoes in a strainer set over a large bowl (A) and gently squeeze; reserve the liquid in bowl A and leave the strainer over the bowl. Place the squeezed potato in a separate bowl (B), add enough water to cover (about 2 cups), swirl the potatoes around to rinse, and pour the potatoes back into the strainer over bowl A, saving the liquid in bowl A. Squeeze the potatoes a second time. Place the squeezed potatoes back into empty bowl B. Let the liquid in bowl A sit for about 20 minutes, so the potato starch can settle to the bottom.

Tip bowl A to pour away as much liquid from it as possible, while leaving the starch at the bottom of the bowl. Add the reserved potatoes from bowl B to the starch in bowl A. Mix well to combine and season with about ½ teaspoon of salt.

Heat about 1 tablespoon of the oil in a heavy-bottomed skillet over medium-high heat; the oil should dance and sizzle. Divide the batter into thirds and make one pancake at a time, using about 1 tablespoon of oil per pancake. When the bottom turns golden brown, about 4 minutes, flip and cook for another 3 minutes. Repeat with the remaining batter and oil. Serve with Soy-Vinegar Dipping Sauce or Everyday Korean All-Purpose Sauce. Any leftovers can be reheated in a dry skillet.

KIMCHI PANCAKES

Kimchi Jeon

Of all the ways to enjoy kimchi, this is probably one of our very favorite preparations to use up the last bit before starting in on a new batch. **MAKES 3 PANCAKES**

2 cups kimchi, store-bought or homemade (page 134), squeezed and chopped

½ cup kimchi juice (from 2 cups of kimchi)

½ cup water or broth

1 cup all-purpose flour

½ cup ground pork or bacon or ham or shrimp (optional)

3 to 5 tablespoons neutral oil, such as canola or grapeseed

FOR SERVING Soy-Vinegar Dipping Sauce (page 21) or another favorite sauce

Squeeze the kimchi over a medium-size bowl to remove any excess liquid (try to get about ½ cup), reserving the liquid in the bowl. Chop the squeezed kimchi and set it aside. Add the water and flour to the reserved kimchi juice and whisk until smooth. Add the chopped kimchi.

Heat about 1½ tablespoons of the oil in a heavy-bottomed skillet over medium-high heat; the oil should dance and sizzle. Start by adding one-third of the batter to the pan; spread evenly to form a round pancake. While sizzling, top evenly with one-third of the pork, if using. If the pancake is steaming and not sizzling, increase the heat and add another drop of oil. When the pancake crisps up and the bottom starts to turn golden, about 4 minutes, flip and cook the other side until golden and crisp, about 2 minutes. Add 1 to 2 teaspoons of oil if the pan appears dry. Repeat with the remaining batter and pork, if using. Let the cooked pancakes cool slightly on a wooden cutting board or paper towel–lined cookie sheet. Slice into wedges and serve with Soy-Vinegar Dipping Sauce. Any leftovers can be reheated in a dry skillet.

PANFRIED STUFFED VEGETABLES

Modeum Jeon

These stuffed, lightly battered, and panfried vegetables are synonymous with festivals and holidays, especially Chuseok (Korean Thanksgiving) and the lunar new year. The day before big holidays, the entire house fills with the scent of frying vegetables. This dish was traditionally intended as an offering to the ancestors, so cooks always guard their kitchen in case any sneaky family members come in to steal a few pieces. If you have leftover filling after stuffing the vegetables, form into patties or small meatballs and panfry along with the vegetables. This is the Korean equivalent to the meatballs commonly found in lunch boxes or served as traditional *anju* (bar food) to accompany rice wines; children and adults alike adore this dish. If you want to make these vegetarian, replace the meat with sautéed minced mushrooms or tempeh. And for extra flavor, use duck fat or beef tallow in place of vegetable oil. **MAKES 8 TO 10 APPETIZER SERVINGS**

FOR THE FILLING

1 pound firm tofu

1 pound ground pork or beef

1 large egg, lightly beaten

1 teaspoon fine sea salt

½ teaspoon freshly ground black pepper

3 tablespoons minced shallot

¼ cup finely diced carrot

¼ cup finely chopped chives

FOR THE VEGETABLES AND FRYING

10 jalapeño peppers

12 to 15 fresh shiitake mushrooms (preferably Chinese shiitake) or cremini mushrooms

2 small yellow or white onions

About 1 cup all-purpose flour, for dredging and dusting

4 large eggs

Neutral oil, such as grapeseed or canola, for shallow panfrying

FOR SERVING Soy-Vinegar Dipping Sauce (page 21)

Make the filling: Place the tofu on a plate and place the plate in the sink. Set a cutting board on top of the plate to press and drain out the liquid (about 1 hour; drain frequently). If in a hurry, cut the tofu in half and microwave on HIGH for 30 seconds.

Place the drained tofu on paper towels (or a dish towel) and press gently on the tofu to release any excess liquid, then hand crush the tofu into a large bowl. (You can also press the tofu through a fine-mesh sieve for a finer-grained tofu.) Add the pork, egg, salt, black pepper, shallot, carrot, and chives. Mix gently so the ingredients are just combined, being careful not to overmix; set aside.

Prep the vegetables: Cut the jalapeños lengthwise, remove the seeds but leave on the stems so that the stuffing doesn't fall out. Trim the stems from the shiitake mushrooms; using a small teaspoon, gently scoop out some of the inside of the cap, being careful not to tear the cap, to make room for the stuffing. Peel and slice the onions horizontally into slices about ½ inch thick. Select two or three onion rings together (best from the ends of the onions) that form a little cup and are similar in size or a little smaller than the mushroom caps. Save any leftover rings for another use (e.g., fried onion rings, fried rice, or broth).

Once the vegetables are prepped, lightly dust inside them with flour, which will help the stuffing adhere better to the vegetables. Stuff the vegetables with the filling mixture. These are best eaten when made the same day, but the vegetables can be prepped and stuffed to this point (see note). Cover and refrigerate for up to 4 hours ahead.

Place 1 cup of flour on a shallow plate or bowl. Beat the eggs in a separate bowl to make an egg wash. Heat a nonstick or a well-seasoned cast-iron skillet over medium-high heat. Pour in about 2 tablespoons of the vegetable oil.

Coat the stuffed vegetables with flour, then dip in the egg wash. When the oil is hot but not quite smoking, add a few stuffed vegetables at a time, being careful not to overcrowd the pan. When cooking the jalapeños and mushrooms, place them, filling side down, in the pan and cook until mostly finished, 3 to 4 minutes. Turn and cook for another 3 minutes. If the vegetables are starting to brown too quickly, lower the heat slightly. Drain the fried vegetables on a paper towel–lined plate or cooling rack (traditionally Korean cooks will drain these on a woven bamboo basket to prevent condensation and sogginess). Add another 2 tablespoons of oil to the pan and let heat until hot but not smoking. Cook the remaining vegetables, in batches as needed. These are best served hot with Soy-Vinegar Dipping Sauce.

NOTE: These are best eaten the day they're made, but the vegetables can be fried one day in advance. Let cool and store, covered, in the refrigerator; gently reheat in a dry, nonstick pan over medium heat. Because the vegetables were panfried with oil, when heated, the excess oil will help them crisp up.

BUTTERNUT SQUASH PANCAKES
Ddangkong Hobak Jeon

You can make this with any winter squash, such as butternut, acorn, or kabocha. Because of the natural sweetness in squash, children tend to go for these as soon as they come out of the pan, so make extra. For a lighter version, try thin wedges of squash dredged in flour, dipped in egg wash, and then panfried, similar to Oyster Fritters (page 42).

MAKES 15 TO 18 MINI PANCAKES

1 cup all-purpose flour

1 large egg

1 cup water

1 teaspoon fine sea salt

3 cups squash, such as butternut, acorn, or kabocha, peeled, seeded, and julienned or cut into thin matchsticks

2 tablespoons chopped fresh chiles, such as jalapeño or serrano (optional)

6 tablespoons neutral oil, such as canola or grapeseed

FOR SERVING Soy-Vinegar Dipping Sauce (page 21) or other favorite dipping sauce

Place the flour, egg, water, and salt in a large bowl and whisk to combine. Fold in the butternut squash and chiles, if using. Heat a large, heavy-bottomed pan or cast-iron skillet over medium-high heat. Add 2 tablespoons of the oil, and when the oil is hot—it should dance a little and sizzle but not smoke—add the batter, about ¼ cup at a time, to make about six mini pancakes total. When the bottom browns (after about 3 minutes), flip and continue to cook the other side for another 2 minutes, or until golden and cooked through. If the pancake is steaming and not sizzling, increase the heat and add another drop of oil. Repeat with the remaining batter. Serve immediately with Soy-Vinegar Dipping Sauce. Any leftovers can be reheated in a dry skillet.

OYSTER FRITTERS

Gul Jeon

This is a perfect appetizer to make when dinner is running late; it's quick, best consumed hot, and great for feeding hungry folks hanging out in the kitchen. The light batter really lets the freshness of the oysters shine. This same method can be used to feature everything from thin slices of zucchini and acorn squash to almost anything you would fry with a light batter. **MAKES ABOUT 4 APPETIZER SERVINGS**

12 to 16 shucked, preferably large oysters

1 cup all-purpose flour

2 large eggs, lightly beaten

¼ cup neutral oil, such as grapeseed or canola, for frying

Salt and freshly ground black pepper

FOR SERVING Soy-Vinegar Dipping Sauce (page 21)

Pick through and discard any shells from the oysters; pat dry. Place the flour in a shallow plate, and the eggs in a large, shallow bowl. Heat a medium-size skillet over medium-high heat. Add the oil.

When the oil is hot (not smoking but starting to dance around), dredge the oysters, one at a time, in flour, then dip in the egg wash and add to the hot oil. The batter should bubble and sizzle right away; otherwise, increase the heat. Cook for about 2 minutes, or until the bottom starts to turn golden brown. If browning too quickly or not quickly enough, lower or increase the heat accordingly. Gently flip and cook the other side for another 1 minute. Place on a paper towel–lined plate to drain any excess oil. Season, if desired, with a little salt and pepper hot out of the fryer and serve at once with Soy-Vinegar Dipping Sauce.

EGG PINWHEELS WITH SEAWEED

Gyeranmari

Often part of the copious *banchan* offerings, this egg pinwheel is a nice anytime snack or part of a brunch. Just as when making crepes, use a reliable nonstick pan. Adding the batter in batches as you go and sliding the rolled side to the edge of the pan, allows the eggs to not overcook. It's okay if the pinwheel is not rolling perfectly early on; as long as you get the very last flip, it's all good. **MAKES 3 TO 4 SERVINGS AS AN APPETIZER**

3 large eggs

1 teaspoon fish sauce, ¼ teaspoon fine sea salt, or 1 teaspoon of soy sauce

½ teaspoon sesame oil

1 tablespoon finely diced carrot

1 tablespoon finely chopped chives or green onion

1 tablespoon neutral oil, such as grapeseed or canola

6 to 8 small sheets of roasted seaweed snack or thinly sliced perilla leaves or other fresh herb leaves

Place the eggs, fish sauce, and sesame oil in a medium-size bowl; whisk gently to combine. Add the carrot and chives.

Heat an 8-inch nonstick pan over medium-high heat. Add some of the oil to coat the pan evenly. Lower the heat to medium-low. Pour half of the egg mixture into the pan to make a thin, crepelike layer, tipping and turning the pan so the eggs spread evenly across the bottom. Place half of the seaweed on top of the egg mixture. Once the eggs just start to firm up, about 45 seconds, using a heatproof flexible spatula, start to roll the omelet from the right to the middle and roll halfway into a tight log. (If you're left-handed, start rolling from the opposite side.) Slide the egg log to the right edge of the pan. If there's not enough oil, add a little more oil to the pan. Tilt the pan slightly to the left and gently pour in half of the remaining egg mixture into the left side of the pan, which will blend into the unrolled portion of the log. Place pan evenly over the heat and let cook for another minute, add the seaweed, and repeat with the remaining egg mixture. Place the log, seam side down, on a wooden cutting board to cool for about 2 minutes before slicing into approximately 1-inch-thick pinwheels.

RICE BALLS WRAPPED IN LEAFY GREENS

Ssambap

These small seasoned rice balls wrapped in leafy greens were inspired by Jungsik, a two–Michelin star restaurant in New York City, where they are served as an amuse-bouche. For the sausage, we use *lap cheong*, a type of Chinese sausage, which yields an earthy sweetness. You can try instead chopped leftover Beef Bulgogi Meatballs (page 161), L.A.-Style Kalbi (page 154), or ground beef seasoned with soy, brown sugar, and garlic. If you don't have sweet rice readily available, feel free to make rice balls, using regular short-grain rice, as in our Pork Belly and Green Onion One-Pot Rice recipe (page 205). **MAKES 4 TO 6 SERVINGS AS AN HORS D'OEUVRE**

2 cups uncooked sticky rice (a.k.a. sweet or glutinous rice)

2¼ cups water or chicken broth, preferably homemade

1 tablespoon sesame oil

1 tablespoon low-sodium soy sauce

3 to 4 links *lap cheong*, sliced (optional; see headnote)

4 dried shiitake mushroom caps, soaked, then thinly sliced

2 tablespoons thinly sliced fresh ginger

20 large leaves of your choice, such as beet, pumpkin, perilla, cabbage, or chard (about 5 inches wide)

FOR SERVING Ssamjang (page 20), Soy-Vinegar Dipping Sauce (page 21), or Salted Shrimp Lemon Aioli (page 22)

Make the rice: Rinse the sticky rice and place in a bowl with water or broth to cover (about 2¼ cups), and let sit for at least 2 hours and up to overnight. Place the sticky rice plus any remaining water from soaking, and the sesame oil, soy sauce, sausage, mushroom, and ginger in a medium-size to large pot with tight-fitting lid. Place over high heat and bring to a boil, then lower the heat to medium-low to low and stir. When the liquid is just gently simmering—a few small bubbles will appear on the surface—cover and let cook without disturbing for 18 minutes. Remove from the heat and let sit for 5 minutes. Uncover and let cool. If making rice wraps and not serving on lettuce leaves or a spoon (see serving suggestion below), blanch the leaves while the rice is cooling.

To prepare the leaves: Plunge the leaves in a large pot of lightly salted boiling water and cook 2 to 4 minutes, depending on the thickness of the leaf, until the leaves are tender and pliable but not soft and mushy. Using a slotted spoon, transfer the leaves from the boiling water to a large bowl of ice water. Let cool and then drain the leaves thoroughly. Pat dry to remove any liquid; cut off and discard any tough stems. If the leaves are large, you can trim to 4 to 5 inches in diameter.

When the rice is cool enough to handle, form into 20 to 25 rice balls about 1 inch in diameter. Place a rice ball and a dollop of *ssamjang* in the center of a leaf and roll to enclose the rice. Repeat with the remaining leaves and rice balls.

SERVING SUGGESTION: Make the rice balls and serve on a fresh lettuce leaf on a platter and let guests help themselves to various sauces. Or serve on small porcelain spoons dotted with *ssamjang* for a single bite.

VEGETABLE CRUDITÉS
WITH DIPPING SAUCES

Koreans make *ssam* with fresh leafy greens, such as lettuce, perilla, beet, chard, and chicory, and always have sliced vegetables, such as cucumbers, carrots, and chiles to dip in *ssamjang*. We added our own *Everyday Korean* spin on the dipping sauces to include, with a nod to Provence, Anchovy-Perilla Anchoiade (page 24) and Salted Shrimp Lemon Aioli (page 22), and Gochujang Sour Cream (page 22). You could also include a small bowl of Miso Crema (page 24). Serve as a fresh, seasonal starter for dinner parties, as part of a picnic assortment, or a light main course.

MAKES 6 TO 10 SERVINGS

6 cups fresh seasonal vegetables, such as radishes, carrots, cucumber, snap peas, or cherry tomatoes

2 cups blanched vegetables, such as broccoli, cauliflower, or green beans (see note)

½ pound fingerling potatoes, boiled, or leftover Candied Baby Potato Banchan (page 99)

6 large soft-boiled eggs, halved (see note)

1 cup Gochujang Sour Cream (page 22)

1 cup Ssamjang (page 20)

1 cup Salted Shrimp Lemon Aioli (page 22)

1 cup Anchovy-Perilla Anchoiade (page 24)

FOR SERVING Soy-Vinegar Dipping Sauce (page 21) or other favorite dipping sauce

Slice the vegetables into matchsticks and some into bite-size pieces, depending on the vegetable. Arrange the fresh and blanched vegetables, boiled potatoes, and eggs on a large platter. Serve with the dipping sauces of your choice.

TO MAKE SOFT-BOILED EGGS: Bring a pot of water to boil over high heat. Gently lower the eggs into the water and let the water come back to a low boil. Lower the heat to medium-high and set a timer for 6 minutes 15 seconds. When ready, immediately remove the pot from the heat and run the eggs under cool water. Peel.

TO BLANCH THE VEGETABLES: Have ready a large bowl of ice water. Plunge the vegetables, one kind at a time, in a large pot of lightly salted boiling water and cook for 2 to 4 minutes, depending on the thickness of the vegetable, until just tender but not soft or mushy. Using a slotted spoon, transfer the vegetables from the boiling water to the ice water. Let cool and then drain thoroughly.

KOREAN-STYLE BEEF TARTARE
WITH ASIAN PEAR

Yukhoe

Many think of steak tartare as a restaurant dish and not something to attempt at home. But it's so simple and delicious that we urge you to try it. Our version is lightly seasoned with soy sauce and sesame oil and served on a bed of crunchy, sweet Asian pears. It's luscious as is, but if you'd like an additional garnish, serve with toasted seaweed to make steak tartare "wraps" or "tacos."

As for those worried about bacteria, the most important thing is the *quality* of the meat you are choosing. So, go to a trusted butcher and get the highest-quality leanest cut, such as top round or eye of round or beef tenderloin, that you can find. And keep in mind that if you are pregnant or have a weakened immune system, it's best to avoid eating raw or undercooked meat, shellfish, poultry, and eggs altogether. **MAKES 3 TO 4 SERVINGS, AS AN APPETIZER (ABOUT 2 CUPS)**

½ pound lean beef, preferably top round or eye of round or beef tenderloin

2 tablespoons granulated sugar

1 teaspoon fresh lemon juice

½ medium-size Asian pear, sliced into matchsticks about ⅛ inch thick by 2½ inches long

1 tablespoon low-sodium soy sauce

1 tablespoon sesame oil

1 tablespoon minced green onion, white parts

½ tablespoon minced garlic

¼ teaspoon fine sea salt

¼ teaspoon freshly ground black pepper

OPTIONAL GARNISHES 1 tablespoon pine nuts, minced; ½ teaspoon toasted sesame seeds; 1 fresh quail egg yolk per person or 1 chicken egg yolk for a family-style plate

FOR SERVING fried wonton chips, toasted seaweed, hot cooked rice

Rinse and pat dry the meat; place in the freezer to chill for 2 to 3 hours. This will help you slice it neatly.

Combine 1 cup of ice-cold water with 1 tablespoon of the sugar and lemon juice in a small bowl and soak the pear matchsticks.

Slice the beef along the grain into matchsticks (about ⅛ inch thick by 2½ inches long) for a traditional presentation, or in small cubes for a modern one. Pat dry with a paper towel to absorb any blood. Drain the pears, pat dry, and set aside.

Combine the soy sauce, sesame oil, and remaining tablespoon of sugar, green onions, garlic, salt, and pepper in a small bowl and gently fold in the beef. Mix and toss, using chopsticks or two forks.

Serve the beef over a bed of pears. Garnish, if desired, with minced pine nuts and an egg yolk; (see head-note) swirl the egg yolk into the meat at the table, just before eating. Serve with fried wonton chips, toasted seaweed, or over piping hot rice for *yukhoe bibimbap.*

KOREAN-STYLE FLATBREAD
WITH GOCHUJANG SOUR CREAM

This flatbread is so easy to make and a slam-dunk party pleaser. Some say that Gochujang Sour Cream is the gateway sauce to Korean cuisine. Top this flatbread as you would any pizza, but our favorite is to add slices of heirloom tomato and fresh torn basil. **MAKES 4 FLATBREADS**

4 frozen or fresh store-bought naan

2 cups shredded mozzarella (8 ounces)

½ cup Gochujang Sour Cream (page 22)

OPTIONAL TOPPINGS thinly sliced prosciutto; sunny side-up egg; ground chorizo; tomato and mushroom slices; fresh basil or oregano; Gochugaru-Infused Oil (page 80)

Preheat the oven to 425°F.

Place the naan on a baking sheet. Brush each naan with 2 tablespoons of the Gochujang Sour Cream. Divide the mozzarella evenly among the naan. Top with your favorite toppings. Bake for 10 to 12 minutes, until the cheese bubbles and the naan crisps up.

KOREAN DUMPLINGS THREE WAYS

Mandu

The food world is full of dumplings, pockets of soft dough filled with warm, juicy, lovely bits. Whether you call them ravioli, pierogi, *gyoza*, *baozi*, empanada, pot stickers, kreplach, or *manti*, they are delicious and we love them. There are two classic Korean *mandu* flavors—meat and kimchi. One unique element about *mandu* is the addition of tofu, which acts as a binder and also keeps the filling moist. Here, we use the technique and idea of *mandu* but incorporate everyday flavors, such as peas with ricotta and salmon with cream cheese. Please see the how-to photos (pages 54–56) for pinching and shaping. They don't have to be perfect—it does take years of practice—but it's fun to gather a group and make an assembly line and let everyone pinch and pitch in.

RICOTTA PEA DUMPLINGS

MAKES 45 TO 50 DUMPLINGS

1½ cups ricotta, drained

3 cups fresh English peas, blanched, or frozen peas, thawed

1½ cups grated Parmigiano-Reggiano or Pecorino Romano, or combination of both

1 large egg, beaten

1 tablespoon chopped fresh mint or perilla leaves (optional)

50 store-bought wonton or dumpling wrappers

Neutral oil, such as canola or grapeseed, for panfrying (optional)

Napa cabbage or lettuce leaves, for steaming (optional)

FOR SERVING Soy-Vinegar Dipping Sauce (page 21) or Gochujang Sour Cream (page 22)

Mix together the ricotta, peas, Parmigiano-Reggiano, and egg in a bowl. Blend into a smooth paste using an immersion blender or pulsing in a food processor. Fold in the chopped mint, if using.

Place a dumpling skin in the palm of one hand and add about ½ tablespoon of the filling. Fold in half and make folds to seal (see how-to photos). Or use a fork to press and seal. Repeat with the remaining filling and dumpling skins. Place the dumplings on a baking sheet lined with parchment paper. As you make the dumplings, cover them with parchment paper or a wet cloth to prevent them from drying out. For long-term storage, freeze the entire baking sheet for at least 1 hour before transferring the dumplings to a resealable plastic freezer bag. Keeps in the freezer for up to 3 months. These can be cooked straight from the freezer without thawing first, but the cooking time will increase.

TO PANFRY: Lightly grease a lidded pan with about 1 teaspoon of neutral oil and place the pan over medium-high heat. Place six dumplings, flat side down, in the prepared pan. If using freshly made dumplings, sear for 1 to 1½ minutes; if completely frozen, cook for another 1 to 1½ minutes, until the bottom of each dumpling turns golden brown. Lower the heat to medium-low to low, add 1 tablespoon of water, and cover at once with a tight-fitting lid. (This step requires some speed so you don't get splashed when the oil meets the water, and is an essential step in fully cooking the filling.) If using fresh, let steam for another 2 minutes; if using frozen, cook for an additional 3 to 4 minutes. (The total cooking time for fresh dumplings is 3 to 4 minutes; for frozen dumplings, 6 to 7 minutes.) Serve immediately with Soy-Vinegar Dipping Sauce or Gochujang Sour Cream.

TO STEAM: Boil water in a pot that fits your steamer, line the steamer with napa cabbage or lettuce leaves, and place the dumplings on the leaves so they don't touch one another. Cover. Steam for 10 minutes. Serve immediately with Soy-Vinegar Dipping Sauce.

SMOKED SALMON DUMPLINGS
MAKES 45 TO 50 DUMPLINGS

2 cups chopped smoked salmon

1 cup cream cheese (4 ounces)

1 cup grated Parmigiano-Reggiano

1 cup ricotta, drained, or tofu, drained and crumbled

1 large egg, beaten

½ cup chopped chives

2 jalapeño peppers, chopped (optional)

50 store-bought wonton or dumpling wrappers

Neutral oil, such as canola or grapeseed, for panfrying (optional)

Napa cabbage or lettuce leaves, for steaming (optional)

FOR SERVING Soy-Vinegar Dipping Sauce (page 21) or Gochujang Sour Cream (page 22)

Mix together the salmon, cream cheese, Parmigiano-Reggiano, ricotta, egg, chives, and jalapeños, if using, in a small bowl.

Place a dumpling skin in the palm of one hand and add about ½ tablespoon of the filling. Fold in half and make folds to seal (see how-to photos, pages 54–56). Or use a fork to press and seal. Repeat with the remaining filling and dumpling skins. Place the dumplings on a baking sheet lined with parchment paper. As you make the dumplings, cover them with parchment paper or a wet cloth to prevent them from drying out. For long-term storage, freeze the entire baking sheet for at least 1 hour before transferring the dumplings to a resealable plastic freezer bag. Keeps in the freezer for up to 3 months. These can be cooked straight from the freezer without thawing first, but the cooking time will increase.

TO PANFRY: Lightly grease a lidded pan with about 1 teaspoon of neutral oil and place the pan over medium-high heat. Place six dumplings, flat side down, in the prepared pan. If using freshly made dumplings, sear for 1 to 1½ minutes; if completely frozen, cook for another 1 to 1½ minutes, until the bottom of each dumpling turns golden brown. Lower the heat to medium-low to low, add 1 tablespoon of water, and cover at once with a tight-fitting lid. (This step requires some speed so you don't get splashed when the oil meets the water, and is an essential step in fully cooking the filling.) If using fresh, let steam for another 2 minutes; if using frozen, cook for an additional 3 to 4 minutes. The total cooking time for fresh dumplings is 3 to 4 minutes; for frozen dumplings, 6 to 7 minutes. Serve immediately with Soy-Vinegar Dipping Sauce or Gochujang Sour Cream.

TO STEAM: Boil water in a pot that fits your steamer, line the steamer with napa cabbage or lettuce leaves and place the dumplings on the leaves so they don't touch one another. Cover. Steam for 10 minutes. Serve immediately with Soy-Vinegar Dipping Sauce.

FOCACCIA WITH FRIED KIMCHI

Inspired by the beloved British author and food columnist Nigel Slater's recipe for Focaccia with Olives. Here we've tamed the funk of kimchi in butter and added it as a topping. Try sliced mushrooms and cheese or green onions. This is an absolute crowd-pleaser and pleasantly surprises even the most ardently kimchi-shy folks. Serve as a stand-and-snack option for guests when they arrive or as part of a larger meal, such as the braised short ribs, to soak up all the braising liquid. **MAKES 8 TO 10 SERVINGS AS PART OF A MEAL**

4 cups all-purpose or bread flour

1½ teaspoons fine sea salt

2 teaspoons fast-acting yeast (or quick-rise or instant yeast)

1 teaspoon granulated sugar

1¾ cups warm water

3 tablespoons olive oil

1 tablespoon semolina flour or cornmeal

2 tablespoons unsalted butter

1 heaping cup chopped cabbage kimchi (store-bought is fine)

2 green onions, chopped

1 tablespoon black sesame seeds

Place the flour, salt, yeast, and sugar in the bowl of a stand mixer fitted with the dough hook attachment. Gradually add the warm water. Knead for 5 minutes on medium speed (use settings 4 to 6 on the mixer). The dough will be a bit wet. Cover with plastic wrap or a clean kitchen towel and let rise for 1 to 2 hours, or overnight in the refrigerator. If the dough is refrigerated, let come to room temperature before proceeding to the next step.

Drizzle about 1 tablespoon of the olive oil over a 9-by-12-inch baking sheet (or other oven-safe rectangular baking dish), and sprinkle evenly with the semolina. Scrape the dough onto the baking sheet. Spread the dough evenly in the pan, using your fingers to spread into the corners. It is okay if it doesn't fill the baking sheet entirely. Let the dough rise again for 30 minutes to 1 hour.

Preheat the oven to 425°F. Melt the butter in a medium-size pan over medium heat until just starting to brown and smell nutty, being careful not to let it burn. Sauté the kimchi until the edges start to brown, about 8 minutes. Remove from the heat.

When the dough rises for the second time, sprinkle evenly with the reserved fried kimchi, green onions, sesame seeds, or other toppings of your choice, gently pressing the toppings into the dough. Using your thumb, press about 16 indentations evenly into the dough. Drizzle with the remaining 2 tablespoons of olive oil. Bake until golden brown, 25 to 30 minutes. Let cool just slightly before cutting and serve warm.

FRITTO MISTO
WITH KIMCHI TARTAR SAUCE

Korean street food always includes deep-fried squid cut up with scissors, then drenched in *ddeokbokki* sauce so the breading soaks up all the sweet and spicy goodness. This is a lighter version, brightened with Mediterranean flavors, including thin slices of lemon and plump olives. We love kimchi tartar sauce for this, but you can also serve with our Everyday Korean All-Purpose Sauce (page 25), Gochujang Vinaigrette (page 18), or Soy-Vinegar Dipping Sauce (page 21). **MAKES 4 TO 6 SERVINGS AS AN APPETIZER**

FOR THE FRITTO MISTO

1 pound squid tubes, cleaned, or squid tentacles

8 ounces fresh raw shrimp or bay scallops

¾ cup semolina flour

½ cup all-purpose flour

1 tablespoon baking powder

1 teaspoon fine sea salt

½ teaspoon *gochugaru*, or ¼ teaspoon ground cayenne pepper

2 lemons, 1 thinly sliced and 1 quartered

3 ounces pitted or stuffed olives (optional)

Neutral oil, such as canola or grapeseed, for frying

FOR THE KIMCHI TARTAR SAUCE
MAKES ABOUT 1½ CUPS

1 cup mayonnaise

¼ cup finely chopped kimchi, store-bought or homemade (page 134)

1 teaspoon minced garlic

1 to 2 tablespoons chopped pickled jalapeño peppers, store-bought or homemade (page 116)

1 to 2 pickled daikon radishes (page 116) (optional)

Zest and juice of 1 small lemon, plus more juice if needed

1 tablespoon chopped fresh basil, cilantro, chives, or dill

2 tablespoons rinsed and coarsely chopped capers

Dash of hot sauce or pinch of *gochugaru*

Clean the squid; cut into thin rings if using the tubes; place in a bowl with a few ice cubes, then cover and place in the refrigerator. Peel and clean the shrimp (removing any veins), discarding the shells or freeze them to make stock for another use. Place the peeled and cleaned shrimp in a bowl with a few ice cubes; cover and place in the refrigerator.

Make the kimchi tartar sauce: Combine the mayonnaise, kimchi, garlic, jalapeños, radishes, if using, and the lemon zest and juice, herbs, and capers in a small bowl. Taste and add hot sauce or a pinch of *gochugaru* or more lemon, as needed; set aside.

Whisk together the flours, baking powder, salt, and *gochugaru* in a large bowl; set aside. Drain and pat dry the seafood. Pour enough oil into a large deep pot to be about 4 inches deep. Heat the oil to about 360°F.

Toss the seafood in the flour mixture to coat evenly. When the oil is hot enough (test by adding a pinch of flour or a cube of bread—they should dance and float immediately), add the seafood, shaking off any excess flour, in batches and cook until golden and crisp, 2 to 3 minutes per batch, using a spider to transfer the seafood as it cooks to a paper towel–lined plate. If cooking in batches, make sure to bring the oil temperature back to 360°F between batches. Season lightly with salt as it comes out of the fryer. Toss the lemon slices and olives in the flour mixture and cook until golden and crisp. Serve at once with fresh lemon quarters and kimchi tartar sauce.

FRESH RAINBOW SALAD
WITH PINE NUT VINAIGRETTE

Jat Saengchae

Saengchae, which means "fresh thinly sliced vegetables," burst on the plate and palate with color and flavor. To make this dish an authentic Korean royal court dish, be sure to have five colors that represent the cardinal directions: yellow for center, red for south, black for north, green for east, and white for west. Traditionally, the pine nut sauce would have been mixed, using traditional stone mixers. Here, we mimic the tradition by using a mortar and pestle. If desired, serve topped with cooked, shredded chicken or king crab or steamed or roasted shrimp.

If you have a mandoline slicer with a julienne grater, this will make prep much quicker. Otherwise, enlist someone with good knife skills and patience to thinly slice the vegetables. Depending on what's in season, try switching out some of the veg for apples or crisp peppers, turnips, kohlrabi, jicama, and so on. **MAKES 4 SERVINGS AS AN APPETIZER; YIELDS ABOUT 3 CUPS**

FOR THE FRESH VEGETABLES

½ cup julienned or thin half-moon-sliced cucumbers (English, Persian, and kirby work well)

½ cup julienned or thin half-moon-sliced carrots

½ cup julienned or thin quarter-moon-sliced Asian pear

½ cup julienned or thin half-moon-sliced radish (red, turnips, or daikon)

½ cup julienned onion (optional)

½ cup radish sprouts (optional)

¼ cup thin strips of perilla leaves (optional)

FOR THE PINE NUT VINAIGRETTE

¼ cup pine nuts

2 tablespoons chicken broth, vegetable broth, or water

3 tablespoons rice vinegar or cider vinegar

1 teaspoon yellow mustard (made from powder) or Dijon or whole-grain mustard

¾ teaspoon fine sea salt, plus more if needed

1 tablespoon granulated sugar, if needed

Prep the fresh vegetables: Soak all the julienned vegetables in cold water for at least 5 minutes and up to 30 minutes; this helps the vegetables absorb some of the water and maintain crunch and freshness. If using, soak the onion separately in cold water.

Make the pine nut vinaigrette: Using a mortar and pestle, crush and stir the pine nuts while adding the broth a little at a time to create a creamy paste. Add the vinegar, mustard, and salt; stir. Alternatively, use an immersion blender to blend the vinaigrette until well incorporated.

Drain and pat dry the vegetables. Toss gently with the sauce. Taste and add sugar or more salt, as needed. When serving this for dinner parties, arrange the vegetables on a large platter, drizzle with the pine nut dressing, and toss tableside.

Chapter 3.

A Bowl of Comfort
Soups and Broths

To make a complete Korean meal, a soup or stew must be part of the table. We've included basic broths that you'll use for a variety of recipes, such as the Kelp Broth, which we use not only in the soups and stews, but also in egg custards and one-pot rice. We strongly encourage you to go out of your comfort zone and master these broths to truly understand the delicate nature of Korean flavors. We also added some of our favorite soup recipes for simple weekday dinner options, such as Egg Drop Soup and restorative porridges.

ANCHOVY-KELP BROTH

This crucial broth provides umami to almost all of our soup recipes. Double or triple the recipe and store the broth in mason jars in the refrigerator for up to 10 days or freeze for up to 3 months. It's important to clean the anchovies to allow for a really clear broth that's sweet with no trace of bitterness. You can store dried anchovies in the freezer, but if they get freezer burn, either dry roast them in a dry pan for 2 minutes or microwave for 1 minute. **MAKES ABOUT 5 CUPS**

1½ ounces dried kelp (a.k.a. kombu)

6 cups water

1½ ounces dried anchovies

Soak the kelp in the water in a bowl for about 30 minutes.

To clean the anchovies, first twist off the head and discard; open the belly side to pull out and discard the guts.

Heat a large pot over medium-high heat and toast the anchovies to remove any fishiness, about 2 minutes. Add the kelp mixture to the pot. Bring to a boil and lower the heat to a low simmer; cook for 20 minutes. Remove the kelp and anchovies. Store the broth, in an airtight container, in the refrigerator for up to 10 days.

VARIATION: Kelp Broth: Omit the anchovies and make the broth as directed. For Kelp Radish Broth: Omit the anchovies, add ½ daikon radish, and make broth as directed.

DON'T LEAVE ME SOUP

Sahgol-tang

This is a rich beef bone broth that's filling and stores well for several days in the refrigerator and several months in the freezer. As to the name, legend has it that when a husband sees his wife making this soup, he takes it as a sign that she is heading off on a trip, hence "Don't Leave Me" soup. This is definitely one to stick around for on cold wintry days. We make two different broths, one spiked with radish and ginger, the other meaty, and then combine the two. It might seem like a lengthy process, but the actual time required to tend to the broth is less than 30 minutes. Make sure to chill the broth and remove the fat caps (a.k.a. tallow), which can be used to make an extra-flavorful Gochugaru-Infused Oil (page 80) for future use. **MAKES ABOUT 12 CUPS OF BROTH; 4 SERVINGS**

3 pounds beef marrow bones

2 pounds beef knuckle bones with tendon
(if available, otherwise use marrow bones)

1 medium-size daikon radish, or ½ large *mu*
(Korean radish)

Two 2-inch pieces fresh ginger

6 to 8 green onions, including roots

1 pound brisket

6 to 8 jujubes (optional)

Salt and freshly ground black pepper

GARNISHES 2 tablespoons chopped green onion;
cooked noodles, such as mung bean noodles

Optional: Place the bones in a large container and add enough cold tap water to cover. Soak the bones for at least 2 hours and up to half a day, frequently changing the water. Removing the blood helps keep the broth nice and clean.

Rinse the marrow and knuckle bones well, if using, and place in a large stockpot. The bones should take up about half of the stockpot space. Add enough water to cover. Bring to a boil. Cook for 10 minutes. Discard the liquid and rinse the bones under cold tap water; set the bones aside. Rinse the pot.

Place the blanched bones back in the clean stockpot. This time, add extra water after adding enough to cover the bones, about 8 quarts total. Bring to a boil. Add the radish, ginger, and green onions, lower the heat to a low simmer, and let simmer for 2 hours, adding a little more water as it cooks down.

Remove the pot from the heat. Discard the radishes, ginger, and green onions. Reserve the broth (batch A) in a large container; chill for at least 4 hours and up to 24. Pick out the knuckle bones from the stockpot and let cool. When cool enough to handle, and preferably with gloves on, remove the tendons from the bones and reserve in the refrigerator until ready to use; this allows for firm and not mushy tendons. Not all the tendon will be ready to fall off the bone. That's okay; you'll have another opportunity to pick them later.

Put the knuckle bones back in the pot with the marrow bones. Add the brisket to the stockpot, add enough water to cover, and bring to a boil. Lower the heat to simmer again for 2 hours. Let cool slightly, remove the brisket, and add it to the bowl of tendons in the refrigerator. Chill the broth (batch B) in the refrigerator for at least 4 hours and up to 24.

When ready to assemble the soup: Take both batches of broth from the refrigerator, remove the top layer of fat, and place both batches together in a big stockpot.

Remove the brisket and tendons from the refrigerator. Thinly slice the brisket and chop up the tendons; set aside.

Bring the broth to a boil. Add the jujubes, if using, and simmer for 20 minutes. Traditionally, the broth is not seasoned—so that individuals can season on their own—but feel free to season at this point with salt and pepper to taste.

Place the knuckle tendons and brisket slices in a bowl; pour the boiling broth over them. Garnish with green onions and cooked noodles. Serve with a bowl of rice, salt, and pepper. Try the tendons and brisket dipped in the salt and pepper mixture.

NOTE: Triple the recipe for this broth and use for other soups. Store in heavy-duty resealable plastic bags in the freezer for up to 3 months. If you are feeling frugal, make the third batch of broth by adding more water to the remaining marrow and knuckle bones. The broth will no longer be creamy but will still have flavor that can be used in other soups and stews.

FRESH PASTA WITH "DON'T LEAVE ME SOUP" AND GOCHUGARU-INFUSED OIL

This is the type of dish that Seung Hee's grandma would have made had she had an Italian friend over on a rainy day. Grandma always had something boiling on the stove at all times, whether it was chicken backs, pig's feet, or beef knuckles—the secret to her magical flavors—and she would have approved of this dish, especially the *gochugaru*-infused oil, using beef tallow rendered from the bone broth. On its own, the leftover Gochugaru-Infused Oil is good for drizzling over pasta, rice, pizza, and flatbread. **MAKES 1 SERVING**

FOR THE GOCHUGARU-INFUSED OIL
MAKES ABOUT 1 CUP

1 cup rendered beef fat from Don't Leave Me Soup (page 78) or neutral oil, such as canola or grapeseed

3 garlic cloves

1 tablespoon *gochugaru*

FOR THE PASTA AND SOUP

1 tablespoon olive oil

3 garlic cloves, thinly sliced

1 green or red chile, thinly sliced

4 ounces fresh spaghetti-like pasta, cooked for 1 to 2 minutes according to the package instructions

¼ cup beef tendons from Don't Leave Me Soup (page 78) (optional)

½ cup bone broth from Don't Leave Me Soup (page 78) or store-bought

1 teaspoon fish sauce

Juice of ¼ lemon

FOR SERVING 1 tablespoon grated Parmigiano-Reggiano or Pecorino Romano and 1 teaspoon Gochugaru-Infused Oil

GARNISH fresh parsley

Make the Gochugaru-Infused Oil: In a small pot that holds up to 2 cups of liquid, heat the fat and garlic together over medium-high heat until clear. The best way to avoid splattering is to cover the pot with a paper towel (works best if using an electric stove) or a splatter guard. When the garlic has turned golden brown, 3 to 4 minutes, turn off the heat. Add the *gochugaru*; it will bubble up at first and the *gochugaru* will turn brown. Chill, then strain through cheesecloth into a mason jar. Discard the solids. Keeps in the refrigerator for 1 month.

Heat the olive oil in a sauté pan over medium-high heat, and just before it begins to smoke, add the garlic and chile and sauté for about 2 minutes, or just until the garlic and chile start to brown along the edges; be careful not to burn the garlic. Add the cooked pasta, tendons, and bone broth. Stir, using tongs, to get the broth to evaporate and infuse into the pasta. Season with fish sauce and lemon juice. Turn off the heat. Serve with Pecorino, a drizzle of Gochugaru-Infused Oil, and a garnish of parsley.

DRUNKEN MUSSEL SOUP

Honghap-tang

This is a popular dish of late-night street carts known as *pocha* in Korea; it is eaten to accompany *soju*. Try this with littleneck, Manila, or steamer clams. If you like, eat the mussels first and save the broth, then reheat it and add cooked vermicelli noodles or rice to the broth and serve with Spicy Quick Pickles (page 116). **MAKES 2 TO 4 SERVINGS**

1 pound mussels, scrubbed and debearded, or clams cleaned and purged of any dirt

3 cups water

1 cup *soju*, sake, or dry white wine (optional)

One 1-inch piece fresh ginger, peeled and thinly sliced

One 2-inch-long piece daikon radish, sliced into chunks

1 serrano chile, stem removed and thinly sliced

GARNISHES chopped fresh cilantro or green onion

Place all the ingredients, except the garnishes, in a pot, bring to a boil, cover, and cook over medium-high heat for about 5 minutes, or until the mussels just begin to pop open, being careful not to overcook the mussels. Gently shake the pot with the lid on, to distribute the heat evenly. Discard any mussels that do not open on their own. Serve immediately with the broth and cilantro or green onion, if desired.

NEW YEAR'S DAY SOUP

Ddeokguk

This classic Korean dish is eaten on New Year's Day. In Korea, it's believed that the day of one's birth, one is already one year old and then everyone ages another year on New Year's Day, so kids, in hopes of an extra birthday, often ask for two bowls of this New Year's Day soup. Delicious straight out of the pot, but reheating the leftovers allows the rice cakes to soften and makes for a silkier broth. **MAKES 2 TO 4 SERVINGS**

2 cups sliced Korean rice cake

4 cups "Don't Leave Me" broth (page 78) or other low-sodium broth of your choice, such as chicken, vegetable, or beef (store-bought Korean bone broth is good, too)

1 tablespoon soy sauce or fish sauce

1 cup cooked brisket or beef tendons from "Don't Leave Me" soup (optional)

½ cup shiitake mushroom caps, sliced (optional)

1 teaspoon minced garlic

½ cup packed chopped green onions

1 large egg, beaten

½ teaspoon sesame oil

⅛ teaspoon freshly ground black pepper

GARNISHES 2 tablespoons chopped green onion, 2 tablespoons crushed toasted seaweed

Soak the rice cakes in 2 cups of cold water for at least 5 minutes and up to 30.

Pour the broth into a large pot over medium-high heat and bring to a boil. Start by adding 1 teaspoon of soy sauce, taste, and add up to 2 more teaspoons. Drain the rice cakes and add to the pot. Add the meat and mushrooms, if using. Simmer for 10 minutes, allowing the rice cakes to absorb the seasoning from the broth. Occasionally stir to prevent the rice cakes from sticking. Add the garlic and green onions and cook for 2 to 3 minutes.

Bring the soup to a boil and drizzle the beaten egg over the bubbling broth to make egg ribbons. Do not stir for 15 seconds, allowing the egg to set. Drizzle with the sesame oil and sprinkle with pepper before turning off the heat. Serve in a bowl and garnish, if desired, with more chopped green onion and crushed toasted seaweed.

EGG DROP SOUP

Gyeranguk

Many think of egg drop soup as a Chinese dish, but Koreans also have a similar soup called *gyeranguk*. It's easy to whip up, especially if you have some broth readily available. The flavors are mellow and don't clash with other dishes. It's also good served alongside Spicy Chicken (page 176). Koreans don't use cornstarch, but Seung Hee, who married into a Chinese restaurant family, discovered the restaurant secrets to this dish: canned chicken broth (Swanson, to be exact), a cornstarch slurry, and frozen corn. Try with and without cornstarch and see which version you like best. We like it with the cornstarch, for a silky texture. **MAKES 4 SERVINGS**

2 tablespoons cornstarch

¼ cup water

4 cups broth, such as Anchovy-Kelp (page 77), kelp broth (see variation, page 77), or chicken broth

¼ cup frozen corn (optional)

2 large eggs, beaten

1 teaspoon fish sauce or soy sauce

Salt and freshly ground black pepper

1 teaspoon toasted sesame oil

GARNISHES green onions or chives

Mix the cornstarch with the water in a small bowl or cup. Bring the broth to a boil in a pot over high heat. Add frozen corn, if using, and cook for about 1 minute. Lower the heat to low. Gently stir in the cornstarch slurry. Increase the heat to medium-high. When the soup boils again, stir the soup vigorously and slowly pour in the beaten eggs. Season with fish sauce and salt and pepper to taste. Add the sesame oil. Garnish with green onions.

FLYING PASTA SOUP

Sujebi

Back in 2008, when we first met, we ate our way through Seoul where we grazed through the city's different neighborhoods tasting everything from soy sauce–boiled silkworms to seasonal blue crabs preserved in soy sauce, rich and thick with crablike jelly. We stopped in one bustling place that specialized in a hand-torn noodle soup. We watched, mesmerized, as the women took balls of pasta dough and swiftly stretched and expertly flung the sheets into a bubbling vat of broth. Think: dumplings or wide noodles softened in a hot broth flecked with sesame, garlic, and green onion. This dough is soft and forgiving, but to save time, you can also use one 10-ounce package of thin wonton/gyoza wrappers or Korean dumpling skins; tear the dough and fling into the soup. **MAKES 4 SERVINGS**

About 3 cups all-purpose flour, plus more for dusting

1 scant cup potato starch, or more all-purpose flour

1 teaspoon fine sea salt

1⅓ cups lukewarm water

8 cups low-sodium chicken broth or Anchovy-Kelp Broth (page 77)

2 tablespoons fish sauce

1 to 2 tablespoons low-sodium soy sauce

2 teaspoons sesame oil

2 teaspoons minced garlic

½ cup thinly sliced yellow onion

1 medium-size potato, sliced into half-moons

1 medium-size zucchini, sliced into half-moons

1 large egg, lightly beaten

GARNISH chopped green onion

Place the flour, potato starch, salt, and water in a medium-size bowl; stir just until combined, then on a lightly floured clean surface, knead the dough into a smooth round ball, 5 to 7 minutes. Wrap in plastic wrap and let chill in the refrigerator for at least 30 minutes and up to overnight. If the dough is refrigerated overnight, let it sit on the kitchen counter for about 20 minutes before using.

Divide the dough into four equal pieces. Using a lightly flour-dusted rolling pin or a pasta maker, roll out each piece to the thickness of lasagna sheets. Dust lightly with flour, if sticking to the counter.

Bring the broth to a boil in a large pot over medium-high heat. Add the fish sauce, soy sauce, sesame oil, garlic, onion, and potato. Boil for 3 minutes. Tear the dough, using your fingers, into about 2-inch lengths and gently fling into the boiling broth. Repeat until all the dough is in the broth. Add the zucchini and let cook at a low boil for another 7 minutes over medium heat. The dough will start to rise to the surface.

Bring the broth to a rapid boil over high heat. Pour the beaten egg into the broth. Let the egg cook for about 10 seconds and then stir. Turn off the heat and serve the soup in warm bowls. Garnish, if desired, with chopped green onion.

GRANDMA'S PUMPKIN SOUP WITH CHILES

Hobak-guk

This clear soup enlists few ingredients so it's important to use the best-quality broth—we highly recommend the Anchovy-Kelp Broth (page 77)—that you can find. As for the squash, an heirloom variety, such as Long Island Cheese or Cinderella, related to butternut squash, is similar to what Seung Hee's grandma used to use. Here we call for butternut as it's more readily available. It's best when the heat from the chiles meets the sweet and tender squash. Stir in fresh young pumpkin leaves when available, otherwise omit or substitute spinach, chard, or kale leaves. **MAKES ABOUT 8 CUPS, SERVES 4 TO 6**

6 cups Anchovy-Kelp Broth (page 77) or good-quality chicken or vegetable broth, preferably homemade

1 pound butternut or Cinderella squash, peeled, seeded, and cut into 1-inch cubes, preferably from the bottom half of the squash

1 tablespoon fish sauce

4 Thai chiles, 2 serrano chiles, or 2 jalapeño peppers

1 cup young pumpkin leaves or other fresh tender greens (optional)

Bring the broth to a boil in a medium-size soup pot over medium-high heat. Add the butternut squash and fish sauce. Cook, uncovered, over medium heat, stirring occasionally, for 10 to 12 minutes, or until the squash is just cooked through. Using a knife tip, poke several holes in one of the chiles and place it whole in the pot. Slice and reserve the other chile(s) for garnish. Stir in the pumpkin leaves or other greens, if using, and continue to cook for about 2 minutes. Remove the whole chile and discard before serving. Garnish, if desired, with the reserved fresh chile slices.

GLAZED LOTUS ROOT

Yeonkeun Jorim

This is a gorgeous sticky crisp vegetable dish that always elicits oohs and ahhs. Lotus root, which is actually the stem of the plant that rises out of the water and blooms into the beautiful sacred flower, is known to help restore balance in the body. Like many other root vegetables, lotus root has a ton of potassium (100 grams contain 556 mg, or 16 percent of the daily value). The texture is creamy and tender, yet crisp and crunchy.

Fresh lotus root is available in the fall, but you can find packages of cut and sliced lotus in the refrigerator section of most Asian markets. When using fresh lotus, it's best to sauté it in a nonstick wok, due to its viscous nature similar to that of okra, but the stickiness will disappear as it cooks. Lotus root tends to turn brown after peeling and slicing, so keep it in water with a splash of vinegar until ready to use. You can also replace the lotus with a few medium-size gold potatoes, cut into matchsticks.

Look for vacuum-sealed fresh lotus root in the refrigerator section of the Asian market. Some specialty stores will also have fresh, raw lotus root, which will need to be peeled and might take up to 10 minutes more cooking time. For more on lotus, see page 245. **MAKES 6 SERVINGS AS A SIDE DISH**

1 pound fresh lotus root, peeled and sliced into ⅛-inch-thick rounds or vacuum-sealed already-sliced lotus

2 tablespoons neutral oil, such as grapeseed or canola

One 1-inch piece fresh ginger, thinly sliced or grated

½ cup water, plus more if needed

2 tablespoons oyster sauce

2 tablespoons soy sauce

2 tablespoons granulated sugar

2 teaspoons toasted sesame oil

2 tablespoons chopped green onion

Make sure to pat dry the lotus with a paper towel so it will be crispy and crunchy instead of soggy. Heat a wok or large, preferably nonstick pan over medium-high heat. Add the oil. Add the lotus root and sauté, stirring occasionally, until the edges begin to brown, about 7 minutes. Add the ginger and stir.

Mix together the water, oyster sauce, soy sauce, and sugar in a small bowl; pour over the lotus root, being careful not to splatter. Cover and let simmer, stirring occasionally, until the liquid is mostly absorbed by the lotus root, about 15 minutes. If the liquid evaporates before the lotus root is cooked, add about 1 tablespoon of water at a time. The lotus root should be tender with a bit of crunch. Remove from the heat. Drizzle with the sesame oil and sprinkle with the green onion. Let cool slightly. Serve as a side dish or an appetizer.

NOTE: Can be stored, covered, in the refrigerator for up to 3 days. Bring to room temperature and serve or, if desired, gently reheat before serving.

SAUTÉED LOTUS ROOT WITH GINGER

Yeonkeun Bokkeum

This recipe is very simple to make but, as a side dish, it provides a satisfying crunch and texture to the overall meal. When using fresh lotus root, it's best to sauté it in a nonstick wok, due to its viscous nature similar to that of okra, but the stickiness will disappear as it cooks. For more on using lotus, see page 245. **MAKES 2 APPETIZER SERVINGS OR 4 BANCHAN SERVINGS**

1 pound fresh lotus root, peeled and sliced into ⅛-inch-thick rounds or vacuum-sealed already-sliced lotus

2 tablespoons neutral oil, such as canola or grapeseed

One 2-inch piece fresh ginger, sliced into thin rounds

3 green onions, white section only, cut into 1-inch lengths

½ teaspoon fine sea salt, or ¼ teaspoon kosher salt

OPTIONAL GARNISHES 1 teaspoon toasted sesame oil, toasted sesame seeds

Make sure to pat dry the lotus with a paper towel so it will be crispy and crunchy instead of soggy. Heat a large wok or sauté pan over medium-high heat; add the oil and let it get very hot, just to about smoking point but not quite. Add the ginger and green onions, sauté for about 20 seconds, and then add the lotus root. Sauté for 10 minutes, until some of the pieces turn golden brown. Season with the salt and garnish, if desired, with the sesame oil and sesame seeds. This is best served hot. Any leftovers can be stored, in an airtight container, in the refrigerator for up to 5 days.

CANDIED
BABY POTATO
BANCHAN

Gamja Jorim

This sticky, sweet *banchan* full of umami crackles like glassy marble and adds a lovely contrast to the other side dishes. It might seem like the sauce will never become glossy, but pay attention toward the end of cooking because once the sauce starts bubbling up, it can quickly burn. If the sauce has become really thick and the potatoes have yet to turn wrinkly, add more broth and continue braising until they do start to look crackled and glazed. The smaller the potato the better, but if you need to cut larger potatoes, make sure to cut them into similarly sized pieces so they cook evenly. **MAKES 1 QUART**

1 pound small new potatoes, about 2 inches in diameter, rinsed

1½ cups Anchovy-Kelp Broth (page 77)

4 tablespoons low-sodium soy sauce

3 tablespoons honey

2 tablespoons mirin

Place the potatoes, broth, soy sauce, honey, and mirin in a medium-size pot over medium heat. When the liquid starts to boil—you'll see small bubbles on the surface—lower the heat to a low simmer. Make sure the potatoes are coated with the sauce and let braise, partially covered, for about 15 minutes. Uncover and cook for another 10 to 15 minutes, turning occasionally, until the potatoes are cooked through and the skins turn wrinkly. Once the potatoes are cooked through, increase the heat and let the sauce bubble and reduce until candied and glossy, about 5 minutes. Can be stored, in an airtight container, in the refrigerator for up to 3 days; gently reheat before serving.

DAIKON RADISH
BANCHAN

Mu Saengchae

Make this dish with turnips or red radishes if you can't find daikon or Korean radishes. When shopping, choose radishes that are firm and heavy for their size. To prep the radish, it's best to use a mandoline slicer set to the julienne setting. Otherwise, cut it into thin matchstick pieces. It's important to mix the *gochugaru* with the vinegar; it actually helps the *gochugaru* to bloom before coloring the salted daikon radishes. **MAKES 3 CUPS, ABOUT 4 SERVINGS AS A SIDE**

About 3 cups peeled and julienned daikon or Korean radish

1 tablespoon fine sea salt

1 tablespoon *gochugaru*

1 tablespoon rice vinegar, cider vinegar, or fresh lemon juice

1 teaspoon granulated sugar

1 teaspoon minced garlic

OPTIONAL GARNISHES ½ teaspoon chopped chives, ½ teaspoon sesame seeds

Place the radish in a bowl, sprinkle with the salt, and let sit for 15 minutes. Combine the *gochugaru*, vinegar, sugar, and garlic in a medium-size bowl. Drain the radish, squeezing out any excess liquid (do not rinse). Add the radish to the *gochugaru* mixture and toss to combine. Garnish, if desired, with chives and sesame seeds. Store in an airtight container in the refrigerator for up to 3 days.

FRESH BEAN SPROUT
BANCHAN

Sukju Namul

This is another simply seasoned *namul banchan* that can be served with any meal. Leftovers can go into savory pancake batters or as rice bowl toppings. **MAKES ABOUT 3 CUPS**

One 1-pound bag fresh bean sprouts, rinsed

½ teaspoon chopped green onion

½ teaspoon minced garlic

1 teaspoon sesame oil

⅛ teaspoon fine sea salt

Pinch of freshly ground black pepper

Bring to a boil a large pot of water (about 6 cups), seasoned with a few pinches of salt, over medium-high heat. Prepare a large bowl of cold water with ice cubes; set aside. Add the bean sprouts and blanch for 1 to 2 minutes. Remove and place in the prepared ice bath. Squeeze out as much excess water as possible from the sprouts, using both hands, being careful not to crush the sprouts. Let drain on a paper towel.

Combine the green onion, garlic, sesame oil, salt, and pepper in a small bowl. Gently toss with the bean sprouts. Taste and add more salt or pepper, as desired. Can be made ahead and stored, in an airtight container, in the refrigerator for up to 2 days.

CRISPY CUCUMBER
BANCHAN

Oi Muchim

Almost everyone we know who has tried this dish loves how crisp and refreshing it is. We call for Persian cucumbers, but if you can find Korean cucumbers, go for it. And be sure to seed any large, thick-skinned cucumber varieties. This is a very simple yet delicious side dish to eat with almost everything. You can easily double or triple the recipe, as needed. **MAKES 4 TO 6 SERVINGS AS A SIDE DISH**

3 Persian or 1 English cucumber, thinly sliced; if the skin is thick, partially peel and remove seeds (12 ounces)

1 tablespoon kosher salt, or 1½ tablespoons fine sea salt

2 green onions, white and some of the pale green parts, thinly sliced

1 tablespoon chopped shallot (optional)

2 teaspoons toasted sesame oil

½ teaspoon low-sodium soy sauce

½ teaspoon minced garlic

¼ teaspoon *gochugaru* (optional)

½ teaspoon granulated sugar (optional)

GARNISH 1 teaspoon toasted sesame seeds

Place the cucumber slices in a bowl. Sprinkle with the salt, toss gently to coat, and let sit for 30 minutes. Rinse the cucumber well under cold water two or three times, then, using your hands, gently squeeze out any excess water. Don't worry if some of the cucumber breaks; pat dry with paper towels to remove any excess moisture.

Place the squeezed cucumbers, the green onions, shallot, if using, sesame oil, soy sauce, and garlic in a medium-size bowl. If desired, add *gochugaru*, for added color and spice, plus sugar to taste. Toss well. Garnish with the sesame seeds. Can be stored, in an airtight container, in the refrigerator for 1 to 2 days.

SESAME SPINACH BANCHAN

Shigumchi Namul

The method in making this quick and easy *namul banchan* is to blanch and then lightly season with soy and sesame oil. Make sure to use large-leaf spinach, not baby spinach. This recipe works well with just about any leafy green and is a great way to make use of fresh beet greens or radish greens that are often discarded. Experiment with Swiss chard, dandelion greens, kale, and bok choy. **MAKES ABOUT 2 CUPS**

2 bunches fresh large-leaf spinach

1 teaspoon toasted sesame oil

1 teaspoon toasted sesame seeds

½ to 1 teaspoon finely chopped green onion

½ to 1 teaspoon minced garlic

1 teaspoon low-sodium soy sauce

Salt and freshly ground black pepper

Bring to a boil a large pot of water (about 6 cups), seasoned with a few pinches of salt, over medium-high heat. Wash the spinach thoroughly to remove any dirt from the stems; keep the stems intact. Prepare a large bowl of cold water with ice cubes; set aside.

Add the spinach to the boiling water and cook for 1 to 2 minutes; remove the leaves and place in the prepared ice bath. Drain the spinach and squeeze the water from the leaves, using both hands, and remove as much of the water as possible while being careful not to smash the leaves too much. Pat dry with paper towels to remove any excess moisture.

Combine the sesame oil, sesame seeds, green onion, garlic, and soy sauce in a small bowl. Toss with the blanched spinach and season to taste with salt and pepper. Can be made ahead and stored, covered, in the refrigerator, for up to 2 days.

LEAFY GREENS WITH GOCHUJANG

Namul Gochujang Muchim

This is a basic recipe for a spicy leafy green *namul banchan*. Quickly blanch the greens of your choice—dandelion, chard, spinach, beet greens, mustard greens, turnip greens, collards—then toss with Gochujang Vinaigrette (page 18) and a tad more sesame oil and minced garlic. Serve on top of any rice bowls or as part of the larger meal. It's simple, quick, and delicious. **MAKES ABOUT 1 CUP**

1 bunch leafy greens

1 teaspoon fine sea salt

3 tablespoons Gochujang Vinaigrette (page 18)

1 tablespoon sesame oil

1 teaspoon minced garlic (optional)

OPTIONAL GARNISH ½ teaspoon sesame seeds

Bring to a boil a large pot of water (about 6 cups), seasoned with a few pinches of salt, over medium-high heat. Wash the leaves thoroughly to remove any dirt; keep the stems intact, except to remove any excess or rough stems. Prepare a large bowl of cold water with ice cubes; set aside. When the water starts boiling, blanch the greens for 1 to 2 minutes (1 minute for tender greens, such as spinach or Swiss chard; 2 minutes for tougher greens, such as collards or dandelion). Remove the greens and drain the liquid, place in the prepared ice bath, and then drain again. Squeeze out all the excess liquid. Roughly chop the blanched greens into bite-size pieces.

Combine the Gochujang Vinaigrette with sesame oil and garlic, if using, in a medium-size bowl. Mix well. Add the chopped greens and stir to combine. Garnish with the sesame seeds, if desired. Can be stored, in an airtight container, in the refrigerator for up to 5 days.

NAPA CABBAGE
BANCHAN

Baechu Namul

Koreans eat a lot of napa cabbage mainly in kimchi, but also in soups and stir-fry dishes. This *banchan* uses a similar technique as the other *namul banchan*, such as Sesame Spinach (page 102) or Leafy Greens with Gochujang (page 103), where the vegetable is blanched before it gets seasoned. Here we use *doenjang* to add a robust savory note to the naturally sweet vegetable, but feel free to use miso if you want a flavor that is a bit mellower. **MAKES 4 SERVINGS AS A SIDE**

About 10 outer leaves from 1 head napa cabbage

2 teaspoons *doenjang* or yellow or white miso

1 teaspoon honey or granulated sugar

2 teaspoons rice vinegar

1 teaspoon sesame oil

2 tablespoons chopped green onion

Bring to a boil a large pot of water (about 6 cups), seasoned with a few pinches of salt, over medium-high heat. Prepare a large bowl of cold water with ice cubes; set aside. Add the cabbage leaves to the boiling water and cook for 2 to 4 minutes, until the leaves are just starting to wilt and become pliable. Remove the leaves, using a slotted spoon, and place in the prepared ice bath. Drain the leaves and pat dry with paper towels to remove any excess moisture. Chop the leaves and place in a medium-size bowl. Add the miso, honey, vinegar, sesame oil, and green onion. Toss to combine well. Can be stored, in an airtight container, in the refrigerator for up to 5 days.

SHIITAKE MUSHROOM
BANCHAN

Pyogo Buseot Bokkeum

Pyogo buseot, a.k.a. shiitake mushrooms, are highly regarded—they can be very pricey—in Korean cuisine, similar to that of French cèpe or Italian porcini. Chewy and meaty with an incredible depth of umami, shiitake can easily replace other proteins in many recipes. We love the texture of the dried shiitake that have been reconstituted, but you can also use fresh shiitake or experiment with other mushrooms, such as oyster, hon shimeji, or enoki. **MAKES ABOUT 2 CUPS**

12 dried shiitake mushrooms

1 teaspoon neutral oil, such as canola or grapeseed

2 tablespoons low-sodium soy sauce

½ teaspoon granulated sugar

1 teaspoon minced garlic

1 teaspoon minced green onion

1 teaspoon toasted sesame seeds

1 tablespoon toasted sesame oil

Place the mushrooms in hot water, topping with a small plate or lid so they are submerged; let soak for about 30 minutes. Drain and slice thinly.

Heat the vegetable oil in a nonstick pan over medium-high heat. Sauté the mushrooms for a minute to evaporate the liquid. Add the soy sauce, sugar, garlic, and green onion and sauté for another 3 minutes over medium heat. Turn off the heat and add the sesame seeds and sesame oil. Can be made ahead and stored, in an airtight container, in the refrigerator for up to 2 days.

TOFU JERKY

Treating tofu to a soy sauce bath and baking it in the oven makes for a meaty, jerkylike treat. To get the most flavor, really smear the spices into the tofu; it's also important to squeeze as much water out of the tofu as you can before you get started. This jerky is good cold the next day or chopped up as a garnish for a variety of noodle and rice dishes.

MAKES 18 TO 20 STICKS

3 tablespoons low-sodium soy sauce

3 tablespoons brown sugar

3 tablespoons Shaoxing wine, vermouth, or sherry

2 tablespoons vegetable oil

1 tablespoon toasted sesame oil

1 teaspoon sriracha (optional)

A few drops of liquid smoke (optional)

1 pound extra-firm tofu, drained (see note)

Cooking spray

Combine the soy sauce, brown sugar, Shaoxing wine, vegetable oil, sesame oil, and if using, the sriracha and liquid smoke in a medium-size bowl. Slice the drained tofu into sticks about 3 inches long by ½ inch thick and add to the marinade. Toss gently to just evenly coat all sides of the tofu, being careful not to break the tofu sticks. Let the marinade seep into the tofu for 30 minutes, occasionally turning to coat evenly.

Preheat the oven to 400°F. Place the tofu on an aluminum foil–lined baking sheet sprayed with cooking oil. Brush any remaining marinade onto the tofu, being careful not to let any drip onto the foil, as it will burn on the foil while baking. Bake for 20 minutes, turning the baking sheet once after 10 minutes for even cooking. Turn off the oven but leave the tofu in the oven for another 30 minutes to dry. Can be stored, in an airtight container, in the refrigerator for up to 7 days.

NOTE: To drain the tofu, either cut it in half and microwave on HIGH for 30 seconds, drain the liquid, then pat dry; or place the tofu on a plate and set a heavy object (such as a cutting board) on top, let sit for 1 hour, occasionally draining the liquid, and pat dry.

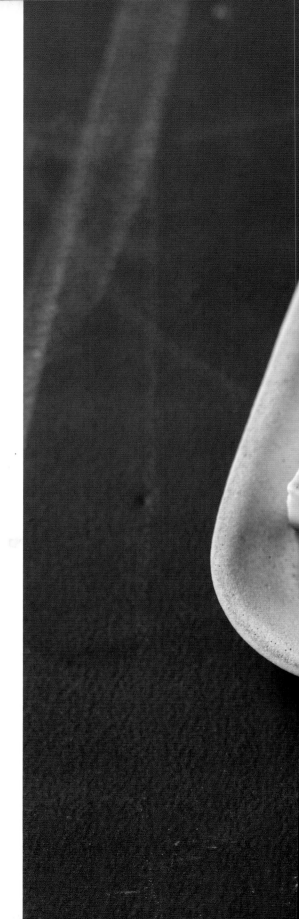

SOFT TOFU WITH SOY VINAIGRETTE

Yeondubu Banchan

This quick recipe is a family-style *banchan* that requires no cooking and is a great way to sneak in plant-based protein. Custardy silken tofu soaks up the soy-vinegar sauce and the crunch from toasted seaweed adds textural contrast. For individual servings, slice the tofu into quarters and divide the sauce equally over them. **MAKES 4 SERVINGS**

One 12-ounce package soft silken tofu

4 tablespoons Soy-Vinegar Dipping Sauce (page 21)

Gochugaru (optional)

1 tablespoon sliced toasted seaweed

1 tablespoon green onion, thinly sliced

Pat dry the tofu with a paper towel to remove excess moisture. Place the silken tofu on a plate. Combine the Soy-Vinegar Dipping Sauce and the *gochugaru*, if using, in a small bowl and pour over the tofu. Top the tofu with sliced toasted seaweed and green onions, and, if using, sprinkle with more *gochugaru*.

HOMEMADE TOFU

Dubu

The nutty flavor alone, not to mention the pure satisfaction of making homemade tofu, is worth the time and effort and doesn't even begin to compare with most store-bought versions. You will need a blender, cheesecloth, and a soy coagulant of your choice, such as lemon juice, cider vinegar, or magnesium chloride (*nigari*). Just so you know, the pressing of the soybeans to release the milk requires some energy, so we like to have a bottle of chilled champagne or a good IPA on hand as a reward for all the hard work. Alternatively, you can use a juicer to do the hard work for you. If you want to add color to the tofu, consider adding 1 teaspoon of ground turmeric or 1 tablespoon of beet juice in Step 4. You can also add a variety of flavors by adding ¼ cup of ground pine nuts, peanuts, or sesame seeds, also in Step 4. **MAKES ONE 12- TO 13-OUNCE PIECE OF TOFU (WEIGHT WILL VARY DEPENDING ON HOW MUCH LIQUID YOU ARE ABLE TO EXTRACT)**

1 pound dried soybeans, preferably organic

2 cups water

2 teaspoons fine sea salt

3 tablespoons fresh lemon juice or cider vinegar (alternatively, use magnesium chloride)

Rinse the dried soybeans and soak overnight in about 6 cups of water. The next day, blend the soybeans with the soaking liquid in two batches, adding ½ cup of fresh water per batch; blend until smooth, adding up to 1 more cup of water total to make a smooth milk.

Bring the soy milk to a boil in a large pot, lower the heat to medium-low, and let simmer for 10 minutes. Line a strainer with cheesecloth and place over a large bowl. Strain the boiled soy milk. Squeeze well until all the liquid is extracted. Reserve the soy pulp for future use, such as in Rustic Stew with Soy Pulp (page 111).

Optional: Use a juicer to separate the milk from the pulp.

Bring the soy milk to a boil again in a medium-size pot, then turn off the heat and add the salt and lemon juice. Gently stir and let stand for 10 minutes. Line a strainer with cheesecloth and place over a bowl. Using a slotted spoon, scoop out the curds. Place the curds in the cheesecloth. Press gently to release any excess water. Place the curd, wrapped in the cheesecloth in a desired mold, or leave over the strainer. Place a heavy object on top and let press for 20 minutes for soft tofu, or 50 minutes for a firmer tofu.

Prepare an ice water bath in a large bowl. Set the tofu in the cold water and let chill for 10 minutes. Drain and use in any recipe that calls for tofu such as Soft Tofu with Soy Vinaigrette (page 106). Store, in an air-tight container, for up to 5 days.

GARLIC SCAPE BANCHAN

Maneul-jjong Bokkeum

These curly pale green stalks, which grow from the bulbs of hardneck garlic plants, come into season in late spring and are often sold in bunches. They are delicious whizzed into pesto, added to compound butter, or grilled along with lemon halves and both tossed together with olive oil and salt. Basically, you can use the scapes as you would garlic cloves. Here we've made a fresh, quick, and easy side dish to feature this seasonal ingredient. **MAKES ABOUT 2¼ CUPS**

1 tablespoon neutral oil, such as canola, avocado, or vegetable

2 cups garlic scapes, trimmed and cut into 2-inch lengths

1 tablespoon *gochugaru* or red pepper flakes

1 tablespoon low-sodium soy sauce

1 tablespoon oyster sauce

1 tablespoon light corn syrup or other sweetener, such as agave nectar, simple syrup, or granulated sugar

½ teaspoon toasted sesame oil

GARNISH toasted sesame seeds

Heat the oil in a medium-size sauté pan over medium-high heat. Add the garlic scapes and sauté for about 2 minutes; add the *gochugaru*, and continue to sauté for another minute. Mix together the soy sauce, oyster sauce, corn syrup, and sesame oil in a small bowl and add to the pan. Cook for another 3 minutes to reduce the sauce until it's glossy and a bit sticky. Turn off the heat and let cool in the pan before serving. Can be stored, in an airtight container, in the refrigerator for 2 to 3 days.

ZUCCHINI WITH SALTED SHRIMP

Aehobak Saeujeot Namul

If you can find Korean squash (similar to zucchini) in your Korean grocery store during the summer, definitely use those, as they have incredible sweetness and a nice firm texture. You can also use pale green Mexican gray squash, also called Middle Eastern or Lebanese squash, which is a summer squash with a smooth shiny skin. The salted shrimp and zucchini flavors go really well together, but if salted shrimp is the only ingredient missing in your pantry to make this, replace with fish sauce or soy sauce. **MAKES 4 TO 6 SERVINGS AS A SIDE DISH**

1 tablespoon neutral oil, such as canola or grapeseed

2 cups zucchini or Mexican gray squash, rinsed and patted dry, sliced into half-moons about ⅛ inch thick

1 tablespoon salted shrimp, including the liquid, or fish sauce

2 tablespoons water

1 teaspoon finely chopped green onion

1 teaspoon minced garlic (optional)

1 teaspoon sesame oil

¼ teaspoon toasted sesame seeds

OPTIONAL GARNISH ⅛ teaspoon *gochugaru*

Heat a lidded wok or a 10-inch nonstick skillet over medium-high heat. Add the oil. Sauté the zucchini until the center starts to turn translucent but not brown, 2 to 3 minutes. Add the salted shrimp and the water and immediately cover the pan. Shaking the pan gently a few times, steam, covered, for about 1 minute. Remove the lid; add the green onion and garlic, if using, and sauté for 30 seconds. Turn off the heat, add the sesame oil, and sprinkle with the sesame seeds. Let the zucchini cool down in the pan for at least 5 minutes before serving. Garnish, if desired, with the *gochugaru*. Can be made a day in advance, but best if consumed the same day. If excess liquid pools at the bottom of the dish, stir to incorporate just before serving.

RUSTIC STEW WITH SOY PULP

Biji Jjigae

Just as used coffee grinds are often free at coffee shops, *biji* (leftover soy pulp) is also free in many tofu-specialty stores in Korea. Seung Hee's grandma made the most comforting foods with what many would consider waste, but she never wasted anything, especially *biji*, after making tofu. She would slowly simmer *biji* with aged kimchi and a few bits of leftover pork in an anchovy-kelp broth to make this rustic and hearty stew that won't win any beauty contests but will always have a top prize for a humble stew with tons of flavor and creamy texture. **MAKES 2 SERVINGS**

1 teaspoon sesame oil

4 ounces chopped pork shoulder or belly

½ cup chopped kimchi (homemade, page 134)

2 cup Anchovy-Kelp Broth (page 77)

1 cup soy pulp, after making tofu (page 108)

1 tablespoon fish sauce or soy sauce

3 green onions, green part only, sliced into 3-inch lengths

FOR SERVING warm rice

Place the sesame oil, pork, and the kimchi in a medium-size pot over high heat and sauté for 3 to 5 minutes, until fragrant and the pork is slightly browned. Add the broth and soy pulp and season with fish sauce. Bring to a boil, then lower the heat and let simmer for 13 to 15 minutes, until the stew has thickened. Add the green onion and simmer for another 2 to 3 minutes. Serve with warm rice.

CANDIED DRIED BABY ANCHOVIES
WITH WALNUTS

Myeolchi Bokkeum

Dried anchovies are essential to Korean cuisine and can be found in Asian markets and specialty markets. The larger ones are usually used to make a broth that is the base of many of our soups, whereas the tiny anchovies are perfect candied, braised, or sautéed as a form of *banchan*. Here, they are candied, which contrasts well with the natural saltiness of the fish. No need to clean the baby anchovies because they are small and sweet as is. **MAKES 1½ CUPS**

1 cup dried baby anchovies (1 to 2 inches long)

1 teaspoon vegetable oil

½ cup walnuts

1 teaspoon low-sodium soy sauce (optional)

2 tablespoons honey

Heat a nonstick wok or skillet over medium heat. Add the anchovies and sauté, tossing constantly, for about 2 minutes. This process helps get rid of any fishiness. Add the oil and walnuts. Sauté for 1 minute, or until the walnuts are heated sufficiently to exude their natural oil. Splash with soy sauce, if using, and drizzle with the honey. Because the pan is hot, the soy or honey will bubble up really quickly, so keep your hands away when the hot steam rises, but shake the wok to coat the anchovies with the honey for about 2 minutes. Let cool in the pan for 5 minutes before serving. Store, in an airtight container, in the refrigerator for up to 2 weeks. Generally this is served cold in Korean households, but if you prefer it warmed, gently heat in the microwave on the DEFROST setting for 1 minute.

TWISTED PEPPER
BANCHAN

Kkwarigochu Bokkeum

These small peppers are great as little bar snacks, appetizers, or to serve as a side dish. Similar to the Spanish tapa *pimientos de Padrón*, Japanese shishito peppers are used here for their twists and turns, which hold the salt and oil in all the right places. While not spicy like serrano or jalapeño, about 1 in 15 can pack a punch, so there's the element of surprise when eating these. This is also delicious made with sliced green bell peppers, or Anaheim or poblano. **MAKES 4 APPETIZER SERVINGS**

1 tablespoon vegetable oil

2 cups shishito peppers or Padrón, whole with stems intact

One 1-inch piece fresh ginger, peeled and sliced

1 tablespoon oyster sauce

1 tablespoon light corn syrup or pure maple syrup (optional)

1 teaspoon sesame oil

1 teaspoon toasted sesame seeds

Heat the oil in a wide sauté pan over medium-high heat until hot but not smoking. Add the peppers and cook, tossing and turning frequently until they blister, about 10 minutes. Add the ginger and toss, then add the oyster sauce and corn syrup, if using; it will bubble up. Stir frequently to glaze the peppers. Once glazed, turn off the heat, drizzle with the sesame oil, and sprinkle with the sesame seeds. Serve warm.

WATERMELON RIND SALAD

Subak Muchim

Koreans like to make use of all the scraps and bits that others might think to toss out, including watermelon rind, which we've turned into a delicious side dish. You can replace with daikon radish or any blanched vegetables, such as spinach, kale, broccoli rabe, or Swiss chard. **MAKES 2 CUPS**

2 cups watermelon rind, thin skin removed, sliced into ¼-inch-thick rectangles

2 teaspoons fine sea salt

1 tablespoon *gochugaru*

1½ teaspoons *gochujang*

1 tablespoon rice vinegar

1 tablespoon agave nectar or granulated sugar

1 teaspoon toasted sesame oil

1 teaspoon soy sauce

Combine the watermelon rind and salt in a small bowl; mix well and let sit for 20 minutes. Rinse under cold water two or three times, then squeeze the rind to get rid of any excess liquid.

Combine the *gochugaru*, *gochujang*, vinegar, agave, sesame oil, and soy sauce in a bowl; mix until well blended. Add the drained watermelon rinds. Serve at once. Can be stored, in an airtight container, for up to 2 days; it will get soggy but it's still okay to consume.

SAUTÉED WATERMELON RINDS

Subak Namul

MAKES 2 CUPS

2 cups watermelon rind, thin outer skin removed, sliced into 3-inch-long matchsticks

2 teaspoons fine sea salt

1 tablespoon neutral oil, such as canola or grapeseed

1 teaspoon minced garlic

1 tablespoon chopped green onion

1 tablespoon broth or water

GARNISH 1 teaspoon toasted sesame seeds

Combine the watermelon rind and salt in a small bowl; mix well and let sit for 20 minutes. Rinse under cold water two or three times, then squeeze the rind to get rid of any excess liquid. Pat dry with paper towels to remove any excess moisture.

Heat the oil in a lidded sauté pan over medium-high heat. Add the watermelon rind and sauté for 3 to 5 minutes, then add the garlic, green onion, and broth. Cover immediately because the liquid can splash. Cook for another 3 minutes, until the liquid has reduced by half. Garnish with the sesame seeds. Can be stored, in an airtight container, in the refrigerator for up to 5 days. Since the rind is sautéed, it will keep longer than the Watermelon Rind Salad (page 114).

FRESH SOY-CURED BLUE CRABS

Kkotge Muchim

Unlike Soy-Preserved Prawns (page 118), which are preserved and can keep for 7 to 10 days, this dish is made to be consumed quickly, within 3 days.

On a cultural note, Korean movies often include marriage proposals with the engagement ring hidden inside the crab shell; the rice-roe mixture is so delicious that marriage is a guaranteed YES! In one popular action film, *My Wife Is a Gangster*, a gang member, as he passes away, tells his lover that he was planning on proposing to her by hiding a ring inside a soy-cured crab shell. It's a scene that makes a lot of Korean women cry.

SERVES 5 TO 6 (1 CRAB PER PERSON)

½ cup Korean soup soy sauce (*gook ganjang*; e.g., Chungjungwon brand), or ¼ cup fish sauce plus ¼ cup low-sodium soy sauce

½ cup low-sodium soy sauce

½ cup filtered water

1 tablespoon granulated sugar

1 tablespoon minced garlic

2 to 3 serrano or Thai chiles, finely chopped (optional)

1 tablespoon rice vinegar or cider vinegar

1 teaspoon ginger juice (from a 1-inch-long piece of fresh ginger; see page 215 for technique)

1 tablespoon *gochugaru*

3 tablespoons chopped green onion

2 tablespoons toasted sesame seeds

5 to 6 medium-size fresh blue crabs (4 to 5 pounds)

Place the Korean soup soy sauce, soy sauce, water, sugar, garlic, chiles, vinegar, ginger juice, *gochugaru*, green onion, and sesame seeds in a large bowl and stir to combine; set aside.

Clean the blue crabs: Scrub the shells with a brush under running water. If the crabs are too active, keep them in the freezer for 1 hour before cleaning them. Using a long pair of tongs, flip each crab over on its back. Hold the crab firmly in the center of the body.

Using kitchen scissors, cut off the main claw. Pull up the crab's abdominal flap or apron and trim it off, using scissors. Separate the lid and the body. Remove the stomach from the lid and set aside. Discard the gills. Using scissors, cut the body, in its shell, into quarters.

Have ready a large bowl or container to store the crab shell quarters; they have all the good roe and tomalley hidden inside. Dunk each shell quarter into the marinade and place in the container. Spoon 1 to 2 teaspoons of the marinade over the stack. Keep in the refrigerator for at least an hour. The roe from the crab shells are best consumed after 1 hour of marinating and within 24 hours; pick the roe and fat from the corners and enjoy with warm rice.

Once the crab shells have been seasoned and stored in the refrigerator, put the rest of the chopped blue crab meat quarters and claws in the sauce. Toss gently and store in a separate airtight container. Cure, in the refrigerator, for at least 24 hours for the body, which is best consumed within 3 days. The claws are best after 48 hours.

Serve the soft crab quarters with the marinade and bowls of warm white rice and toasted seaweed. The body will be soft enough to squeeze the meat out, or pick the meat out of the crab shells. Kitchen scissors work well for some of the hard-to-get sections.

SPICY QUICK PICKLES

Mu Cho-jeolim

This quick refrigerator pickle functions as a palate cleanser among the wide range of flavors in a typical Korean spread. While these pickles pair well with just about any of the savory dishes in our book, we urge you to try them with the Garlic Soy Fried Chicken (page 179). We love including jalapeños or making this with only jalapeños, but they can be omitted if you're not a fan. **MAKES 1 QUART**

1 daikon or watermelon radish, or 2 English cucumbers (about 17.5 ounces)

2 jalapeño peppers (optional)

2 cups water

1 cup rice vinegar, white vinegar, or cider vinegar

½ cup granulated sugar

2 tablespoons fine sea salt or low-sodium soy sauce

Slice the radish and jalapeños, if using, into 1-inch rounds or cubes; place in a clean glass jar.

Place the water, vinegar, sugar, and salt in a medium-size pot over medium-high heat. Bring to a low boil and cook, stirring, for 1 to 2 minutes to dissolve the sugar. Remove from the heat and let cool slightly, then pour the warm liquid over the vegetables in the jar. Cover and let sit in the refrigerator for at least 30 minutes and up to 3 weeks.

VARIATION: Slice the daikon radish paper thin (a mandoline slicer is useful for this) and layer with perilla leaves, stack the layer in a container, then pour the pickling liquid over all. Put a small plate on top to keep everything submerged under the pickling liquid. Refrigerate for at least 1 day before serving. Store in the refrigerator for up to 3 weeks.

SOY-PRESERVED PRAWNS

Saewoo Jang

This recipe was inspired by a soy-preserved blue crab recipe called *gejang*, an addictive spring delicacy, not to be confused with the Fresh Soy-Cured Blue Crabs recipe (page 115). For *gejang*, the crabs are preserved in a marinade that has been strained, boiled, and cooled every 24 hours for 3 to 5 days. Straining and boiling multiple times helps remove any harmful bacteria. *Gejang* is addictive and we weren't sure what could be better until we made these prawns (*saewoo jang*). There's no struggling with a hard shell and the heads are filled with a tomalley so delicious that it makes sucking the heads at the table more than acceptable.

We make this in the summer in Alaska with fresh raw Prince William Sound spot prawns just a few hours out of the water. Firmer in texture than crab, which becomes more like a briny beautiful sea jelly, wild shrimp or tiger prawns could be substituted. Just make sure that they are the freshest available.

As for serving, this dish is also known as a "rice thief"; the soy sauce marinade elicits cries for lots of accompanying rice. This is also so good with soft-boiled eggs and roasted seaweed. We like something green and bite-y, such as green onion, microgreens, pea shoots, or arugula to offset the richness. The whole meal is a hands-on eating frenzy that ends in very happy and satisfied mouths. **SERVES 4 TO 6**

FOR THE MARINADE

2 cups low-sodium soy sauce

2 cups water

¼ cup fish sauce

¾ cup brown sugar

½ cup mirin

1 whole apple, cored and quartered

½ yellow onion

1 lemon, halved

2 serrano chiles

2 dried red chiles

7 garlic cloves, peeled

One 1-inch piece fresh ginger, peeled and thinly sliced into coins

2 green onions, trimmed

FOR THE PRAWNS

1 yellow or white onion, halved, and thinly sliced

2 jalapeño peppers, stems removed, thinly sliced

1 pound large, ultra-fresh raw, shell-on spot prawns or wild shrimp, rinsed and trimmed, and cleaned, if possible, of any veins

FOR SERVING steamed rice, roasted seaweed, soft-boiled eggs, and pea shoots, microgreens, or thinly sliced green onion

Make the marinade: Combine all the marinade ingredients in a large pot over medium-high heat and bring to a boil; let boil for 15 minutes. Strain the liquid into a bowl and discard the solids. Let the marinade cool to room temperature, then chill in the refrigerator or use an ice bath until the marinade is cool enough to add the raw prawns.

Marinate the prawns: Place the thinly sliced onion and jalapeño slices in a single layer in a large container with lid. Add the prawns in a single layer over the onion, then pour the chilled marinade over the prawns. Cover and place in the refrigerator to chill for 24 hours.

After 24 hours, strain the prawns and marinade through a fine-mesh sieve into a pot, reserving the marinade, Place the prawns, onion, and jalapeños back in the refrigerator. Bring the marinade to a boil over medium-high heat and let boil for 5 minutes. Remove from the heat, let cool to room temperature, then chill completely in the refrigerator. Pour the chilled marinade over the prawns, cover the container, and place back in the refrigerator. Repeat the straining, boiling, and chilling process two more times, every 24 hours, for 2 more days.

To serve: Place the prawns on a shallow serving platter and pour the marinade over them; top with the onion and jalapeño slices. Serve with steamed rice, roasted seaweed (*kim nori*), soft-boiled eggs, and pea shoots, micro greens, or thinly sliced green onion.

Chapter 5.

The Heart of the Matter
Kimchi

What exactly is kimchi and how to describe the taste in a single word? This pickled, bubbly taste of Korea can be pungent, salty, spicy, sour, and full of zing from a fermentation process that is essential to our everyday health and happiness. Kimchi offers the complexity and flavor profile to make any cook jump with joy. The sixth flavor similar to umami (*gamchilmat* in Korean) is found in kimchi and offers the rich earthiness of mushroom but is even more satisfying and addictive, thanks to its incredibly varied and multilayered nature—a perfect marriage of salty, sour, sweet, and funky.

Traditionally, many cultures ferment what's available and sustainable. As an agricultural society, preserving food to eat during the winter was crucial to survival for Koreans; they lived off of preserved or fermented vegetables, such as kimchi, and rice that they had harvested in the fall. Although the most common kimchi is made with napa cabbage and radish, just like pickles, kimchi can be made with just about any vegetable. Some regions in Korea make kimchi with dandelion (both leaves and roots), and soybean sprouts.

The best way to enjoy kimchi is to prepare and enjoy it according to the seasons. The classic *baechu* kimchi is made in bulk, and when we say bulk, we mean hundreds of heads of cabbage all salted and preserved just before winter. This event, called *kimjang*, is an important family affair: mostly the women, all sitting around big piles of kimchi paste, wearing elbow-high gloves, massaging salted napa cabbages. This is done in the winter because the cabbages are at their peak.

It is said that winter cabbage is crunchier with fuller heads, whereas summer cabbage is wetter and takes half the salting/brining time required by winter cabbage. The fuller-headed winter cabbages also need more layers of kimchi paste in between the leaves, resulting in a more complex fermentation. Winter temperatures are perfect for a slower fermentation process. Sometimes in the summer, because the ambient temperature is so high, you might find your kimchi fermenting only after half a day, whereas in the winter, kimchi needs a few more days to get zingy.

We encourage you to make a few of these kimchi recipes. Not all are spicy or take a long time to ferment. And not to worry; we are not asking you to bury vegetables for years in and around your backyard. Here you'll find various kimchi recipes, ranging from fresh (unfermented) kimchi slaw to traditional homemade *baechu* and *mat* kimchi.

TURNIP KIMCHI

Soon-mu Kimchi

A classic hassle-free, minimally fermented kimchi from Kanghwa Island, the northernmost island in the West Sea. Kanghwa Island is known for its purple-tipped turnips, which are sweet, mild, and delicious. At farmers' markets, you might encounter turnips that are just a tad smaller than softballs, which work well here. You can also make this kimchi recipe with green or ripe mangoes, or green papayas, and even pineapples. **MAKES ABOUT 7 CUPS**

6 cups sliced purple or white turnips, sliced into half-moons about ¼ inch thick

1 tablespoon fine sea salt

½ batch Everyday Korean Kimchi Paste (page 133)

Combine the turnip slices with the salt in a large bowl or a plastic container (that can hold up to 3 quarts of liquid). Let stand for 10 to 15 minutes. Drain but do not rinse.

Mix the Everyday Korean Kimchi Paste with the salted turnips in a large bowl (that can hold about 1½ gallons of liquid); toss well. Enjoy at once or store, in plastic containers or glass jars with a proper fermentation lid, and let stand on the kitchen counter for 2 to 3 days. After 2 or 3 days, store in the refrigerator. It's best after 7 days, and within 3 weeks.

EVERYDAY KOREAN KIMCHI PASTE

Kimchi Yangnyeum

This kimchi paste is a no-hassle, quick version that you will constantly come back to and different from the one used in Traditional Napa Cabbage Kimchi (page 134). The major difference is the omission of a rice flour paste or gravy. A rice flour paste helps expedite fermentation during the cold months. Also, lactobacillus, friendly bacteria that promotes gut health and grows in kimchi, feeds off the rice flour paste more easily than it does off the carbohydrates in cabbage. It also provides zing, the rightful sign of fermentation that kimchi is alive and healthy. In addition, the paste also helps the *gochugaru* bloom and evenly color the cabbage.

When making kimchi (e.g., Cucumber Kimchi, page 128) during the warmer months, fermentation happens more quickly and there is no need to add the rice flour paste. If you were to add rice flour to cucumber kimchi, it would turn the cucumbers into a mushy mess. The same goes for turnips or cubed radish (*ggakdugi*): there is no need for rice flour; use this Everyday Korean Kimchi Paste instead. It's also good stirred in salad dressings or other marinades. Or tossed with (unsalted) daikon, green mangoes, fresh pineapple, or Asian pear. Make several batches and freeze for up to 3 months. **MAKES ABOUT 2 CUPS**

1 cup *gochugaru*

½ cup fish sauce

½ cup grated Asian pear or apple

2 tablespoons minced garlic

1 teaspoon grated ginger

½ cup julienned daikon radish, cut about 2 inches long

½ cup thinly sliced green onion

½ cup sliced Korean chives, cut into 2½-inch long slices, or chopped shallot or green onion

OPTIONAL ADD-INS

½ grated onion

½ cup Korean mustard greens or Korean chives

½ cup *minari*

1 teaspoon toasted sesame seeds

1 tablespoon pine nuts

1 pint oysters (use if kimchi is meant to be consumed within 5 days)

Mix the *gochugaru* with the fish sauce and pear in a bowl. Allow the *gochugaru* to bloom, 2 to 3 minutes. Add the garlic and ginger; stir to combine. Add the radish, green onion, chives, and any of the optional add-ins, stirring well to combine. Can be stored, in an airtight container, in the refrigerator for up to 5 days.

TRADITIONAL NAPA CABBAGE KIMCHI

Baechu Kimchi

Traditional napa cabbage kimchi is called *baechu "pogi"* kimchi; *pogi* being a unit used to count napa cabbage. It's very common to see all the female members of one family sitting around piles of kimchi paste and hundreds of salted napa cabbage leaves to make kimchi.

In the fall or winter, salting the cabbage properly will take about 8 hours. In the spring or summer, salting might take only 4 to 6 hours. The difference is due to the water content of the cabbage. The best way to test whether your salted cabbage is ready is to choose a leaf with a thick white part closer to the stem end and fold it gently backward. If it snaps off, allow the cabbage to sit for another hour and try again until it bends back gently without breaking.

Recently, many Korean families opt out of *kimjang* and buy kimchi as needed. Most kimchi sold in jars in US supermarkets are chopped napa cabbage kimchi (*mat kimchi*), which is convenient because you can take out how much you want to eat. You can make *mat kimchi* (see variation), which takes a lot less time, and is great when you want smaller batches of kimchi, but just know that it won't age as well as the full-leaf *baechu kimchi*. Lastly, make sure to use food-safe gloves to massage the spicy kimchi paste into the leaves, to prevent your hands from burning for hours. **MAKES 7 TO 8 POUNDS (¾ TO 1 GALLON)**

10 cups water

1 cup coarse Korean sea salt, ¾ cup fine sea salt, or ½ cup kosher salt

5 to 6 pounds napa cabbage, quartered

1½ cups kelp broth (see variation, page 77) or water

2 tablespoons glutinous rice flour (such as *mochiko*)

1 cup *gochugaru*

½ cup fish sauce

3 tablespoons minced garlic

1½ teaspoons minced fresh ginger

½ large Korean pear or 1 medium-size Asian pear, peeled, and seeded, grated

3 cups daikon radish or turnips, julienned

¾ cup sliced Korean chives or green onion, cut in 1½-inch matchsticks

¾ cup sliced *minari*, cut in 1½-inch matchsticks (optional), or add more chives or green onions

Combine the water and salt in a large bowl or a plastic container (that can hold up to 1½ quarts of liquid) and stir until dissolved. Submerge the cabbage in the liquid, making sure that all the leaves are submerged. Lift up some of the leaves so the entire leaf has contact with the salty water. Place a plate or a bowl on top of the cabbage, and place heavy objects such as a bag of flour or rice on top, to keep the cabbage submerged. After 4 to 6 hours, start checking the cabbage by bending backward (see headnote).

Rinse under tap water and squeeze gently, folding the leafy end toward the center of the cabbage. Repeat twice to rinse off any excess salt from the cabbage. Place the squeezed cabbage in a strainer to drain any further excess liquid. Discard the excess liquid and set the cabbage aside.

While the cabbage is brining, place the broth and the glutinous rice flour in a small pot and whisk well. Cook, stirring frequently, over medium-high heat. Once the mixture starts to bubble, lower the heat to medium-low, and continue to cook, whisking, for another minute. The consistency will be similar to that of a thick gravy. Remove from the heat and let cool.

Mix together the *gochugaru* with the fish sauce, garlic, ginger, pear, and chilled glutinous rice flour gravy in a large bowl (that can hold about 1½ gallons of liquid) to create a paste. Fold the daikon radish, chives, and *minari* into the paste.

Place the salted and drained cabbage quarters in a large, separate bowl. Wearing gloves, take about 1 cup of the kimchi paste and rub each leaf with the paste, lifting up one leaf at a time, adding about ¼ cup of the kimchi paste between the leaves. (Don't worry about being too accurate. Also, it's best to place the chunky parts toward the root, where the cabbage is thickest.) Rub the paste all over and then fold the leafy part toward the center of the cabbage. With any loose leaves, wrap the stuffed cabbage like swaddling a baby, to keep all the goodies inside each layer of cabbage. Place the stuffed leaves in a large plastic container. Repeat with the remaining cabbage and kimchi paste. Place any excess leaves on top of the wrapped kimchi to avoid air contact and place plastic wrap over it, pressing the wrap gently onto the kimchi to remove any air.

Fill a clean resealable plastic bag with water and place that in another bag. Place the doubled water bags on top of the plastic wrap to minimize any air contact. Let sit on the kitchen counter or a cool place in your garage for 3 days in the winter or 1 to 2 days during the summer. Check every day to see whether the scent suggests fermentation (a faint sour note). If you are in a cold environment, it will take longer. If your house is warm, it will take a shorter amount of time. Store in the refrigerator for another 2 weeks to slow the fermentation process, and enjoy over the next 4 to 6 months.

NOTE: If not stored properly (where the kimchi has extended contact with air), very rarely but sometimes (and usually after 6 months) a white/pink slime will appear on the outer leaves. Discard those leaves. The inner leaves are fine and make sure to push the kimchi down under the liquid to avoid contact with air.

NOTE: There may be excess kimchi paste left. In this case, you can freeze the paste to use at a later date for kimchi, such as Cucumber Kimchi (page 128), which doesn't require much of the paste.

CHOPPED NAPA CABBAGE KIMCHI
Mat Kimchi

This is the kind of kimchi you'll find in stores, prechopped and sold in jars. It's convenient and much faster to make; it only takes 2 hours to salt the chopped cabbage as opposed to the 8 hours needed for the traditional method. (For more about kimchi, see page 245).
MAKES 7 TO 8 POUNDS (¾ TO 1 GALLON)

10 to 11 cups water

1 cup Korean coarse sea salt, ¾ cup fine sea salt, or ½ cup kosher salt

5 to 6 pounds napa cabbage, chopped into 1½-inch pieces or preferred bite-size pieces

1 cup *gochugaru*

½ cup fish sauce

3 tablespoons minced garlic

1½ teaspoons minced fresh ginger

½ large Korean pear or 1 medium-size Asian pear, peeled, seeded, and grated

3 cups daikon radish or turnips, julienned

¾ cup sliced Korean chives or green onion, cut in 1½-inch matchsticks (about 1 ounce)

¾ cup *minari*, cut in 1½-inch matchsticks (optional), or add more chives or green onions

Mix the salt into the water in a large bowl or a plastic container (that can hold up to 1½ gallons of liquid) until dissolved. Submerge the chopped cabbage in the salt bath. Place a plate or a bowl on top of the cabbage and put heavy objects, such as a bag of flour or rice, on top to keep the cabbage submerged in salted water for 2 hours.

After 2 hours of brining, rinse the cabbage under tap water and squeeze gently. Repeat twice. Place the squeezed cabbage in a strainer to drain any excess liquid. Discard the liquid and set the cabbage aside.

Place the *gochugaru*, fish sauce, garlic, ginger, and pear in a large bowl (that can hold about 1½ gallons of liquid) and mix to combine. Fold in the daikon radish, chives, and *minari*. Add the reserved cabbage (you should have about 10 cups) and incorporate well, using gloved hands. Place in a plastic container, preferably with a tight-fitting lid. Place any excess leaves that might have fallen during the salting process on top of the wrapped kimchi or place plastic wrap directly over the kimchi and press gently to remove any air. To weigh down the kimchi, take one large or several small resealable plastic bags and fill with water; seal well and double wrap by placing the bags of water in another bag. Place these on top of the plastic wrap to protect the kimchi. This helps minimize air contact. Cover with a tight-fitting lid and let sit on the kitchen counter or a cool place in your garage for 3 days in the winter or 1 to 2 days during the summer. Check every day to see whether the scent suggests fermentation (the smell will be slightly vinegary). Store in the refrigerator for another 2 weeks, opening the lid regularly to release air, for slow fermentation, and enjoy for 2 to 3 months. As you eat the kimchi, always cover the surface with plastic wrap so it touches the surface of the kimchi before covering with a lid.

WINTER RADISH KIMCHI WITH CLEAR BROTH

Dongchimi

This is not what most Westerners imagine when they envision kimchi because this winter version is white (as in no *gochugaru*) and brothy. If you find radishes with fresh green tops, add 1 cup of coarsely chopped greens to 6 cups of radishes. You can enjoy at once, but store in the refrigerator for up to one week more for best results. Keep refrigerated for up to three months. If you are making this in the summertime, you can omit the rice flour, which is used to expedite fermentation during the cold-weather months. The addition of pear helps to naturally sweeten the radish over time. If using baby turnips, omit the pear since baby turnips tend to be naturally sweet. Enjoy these vegetables as they continue to evolve, and make sure to sip the broth as it's full of probiotics and deliciousness. **MAKES 4 QUARTS**

2 tablespoons rice flour (optional)

1 cup water (optional)

6 cups sliced *mu* (Korean radish), daikon radish, or small white snow turnips

1 cup sliced radish greens, cut into ½-inch length, preferably from the center of the stem (optional)

3 garlic cloves, sliced

One 2-inch piece fresh ginger, peeled and thinly sliced (about 1 ounce)

1 serrano or jalapeño pepper, poked with a fork

2 green onions, cut into 2-inch matchsticks

¼ cup coarse Korean sea salt, or 3 tablespoons fine sea salt

8 cups cold water

½ medium-size Asian pear, grated (optional)

If making the rice flour mixture (see headnote), whisk together the rice flour and 1 cup of water in a small pot set over medium-high heat; bring to a boil. Simmer for 1 minute while continuing to whisk to avoid clumps. Remove from the heat and set aside to cool.

Slice the radish lengthwise, and then into approximately ⅛-inch-thick half-moons. Place the radish, radish greens, if using, garlic, ginger, serrano, and green onions in a large plastic container. Place 2 tablespoons of the rice flour mixture (if using) in a large bowl, and gradually add the salt and 8 cups of water, stirring to dissolve the salt; add the grated pear if using. (Alternatively, omit the rice flour mixture.)

Pour the salted water mixture over the vegetables, leaving about 1 inch of room at the top. Cover and place the container (or preferred fermentation device, such as mason jars with appropriate lids that releases gas; see note) on a large plate or kitchen towel and let sit on the kitchen counter for 2 days. If it's summer and hot, let sit for 1 day. Bubbles should begin to form on the surface. You can enjoy at once, but store in the refrigerator for up to 1 more week for best results. Keep refrigerated for up to 2 months.

NOTE: It's best to store this in a large plastic bin or mason jars with lids that are appropriate for fermenting foods. Even refrigerated, the kimchi continues to ferment, so if you store in glass, be sure to release the gas every now and then by opening the jar; otherwise it can explode. Enjoy as it continues to evolve.

SPRING WATER KIMCHI
WITH CHILLED BROTH

Mul Kimchi

This *mul kimchi*, which translates to "water kimchi," is served as a palate cleanser between various dishes. It doesn't require long fermentation and is meant to be consumed relatively quickly in order to enjoy the crunch and freshness of the vegetables along with the mild broth. Try including apple, Asian pear, or pomegranate, which will add a fresh, fruity dimension. Because this is not too spicy, Korean parents feed this to their children, while they enjoy the spicier versions. **MAKES ABOUT 1 GALLON**

2 tablespoons *gochugaru*

3 tablespoons rice flour gravy (optional, see previous recipe)

1½ tablespoons fine sea salt (if using Korean coarse sea salt crystals, use 2 tablespoons)

About 8 cups purified water

1 large Asian pear, peeled and grated

2 cups cubed white radish (daikon or Korean), cut into ½-inch cubes

3 cups cubed napa cabbage, cut into ½-inch cubes (use the inner leaves that are yellow)

2 green onions, cut into 1-inch lengths

1 red chile, thinly sliced on the bias

3 garlic cloves, thinly sliced

One 1-inch piece fresh ginger, thinly sliced into coins

5 to 6 dried jujubes (optional)

Place the *gochugaru* in cheesecloth, tie up the cheesecloth, and place in a bowl. Pour 2 cups of water over the cheesecloth. Gently press on the cheesecloth to give a red tint to the water. Discard the cheesecloth and *gochugaru*. Alternatively, place the *gochugaru* in a very fine-mesh sieve and pour the water over it, into a bowl.

Place the rice flour gravy, if using, in a large bowl, pour 2 cups of the *gochugaru*-tinted water over it, and mix

well. Add 1 tablespoon of the salt and add 3 cups of water. Taste the broth. It should taste a bit salty. Add the pear to the broth and mix well. Then, add the radish, napa cabbage, green onions, chile, garlic, and ginger; stir well. Add the jujubes, if using.

Place the kimchi in an airtight plastic container or a fermentation device. If using a mason jar, leave enough space for the gas to escape in the early phase of fermentation. Let sit in a cool place for at least 12 hours (in warm weather) to 24 hours (in cooler weather). Continue fermenting in the refrigerator for another 3 days, checking every day to release any gas. Consume within 14 days for crunchy vegetables and tangy broth.

NOTE: Usually, kimchi will spoil if the broth is not salty enough or exposed to air for too long. The broth will not have a sour (kombucha-like) flavor; rather, a bitter and foul flavor. This rarely happens. The best way to avoid this is to always take out the amount that you will consume in a single meal, to minimize contact with air.

Chapter 6.

The Main Event
Fish, Meat, and Vegetables

Korean traditional cuisine cherishes meat and fish preparations, as those dishes were a sign of wealth and prosperity. Often served family style and consumed to complement rice, just like *banchan*, even the meat-centric dishes, such as L.A.-Style Kalbi (page 154), would be consumed with rice and lettuce to make the meal more abundant. Koreans often cook with the lesser cuts, such as short rib and oxtail, but with a few culinary tricks and marinades, they provide much satisfaction in both flavor and texture. Here, we've honored the Korean love of meat, fish, and seafood while also adapting it to a Western setting.

ROASTED SALMON
WITH GOCHUJANG MAYO

This recipe is inspired by Seung Hee's Uncle Norman, of Japanese descent, who grew up in Hawaii; he makes this for Thanksgiving using a simple recipe of mayo and oyster sauce. We've spiced it up with *gochujang* and garlic and a hint of ginger. This is one of those dishes that's so easy and impressive that your guests will be requesting the recipe. We've had so many friends taste this and immediately start adding it to their weekly dinner routine. The robustness of this dish pairs beautifully with Fresh Quick-Fix Kimchi Salad (page 126). Serve in lettuce wraps with steamed rice.
MAKES 4 TO 6 SERVINGS

Cooking spray (optional)

One 2-pound wild salmon fillet, pin bones removed; skin-on is fine

2 tablespoons mayonnaise, preferably Kewpie brand

2 tablespoons oyster sauce

2 teaspoons *gochujang*

2 teaspoons minced or grated garlic

One 2-inch piece fresh ginger, grated (optional)

FOR SERVING Bibb lettuce and steamed rice, Gochujang Vinaigrette (page 18)

Place an oven rack just beneath the broiler part of your oven. Set the oven to BROIL. Line a sheet pan (a shallow baking sheet) with aluminum foil. Spray lightly, if desired, with cooking spray.

Pat the salmon dry with paper towels. Place the salmon, skin side down, on the prepared pan. If desired, using a sharp knife point, score halfway through the fish lengthwise, and score a few times widthwise; this will help the sauce absorb into the fish.

Mix together the mayonnaise, oyster sauce, *gochujang*, garlic, and ginger, if using, in a small bowl. Brush the sauce evenly over the salmon. Place the baking sheet on the top rack in the oven. Broil, checking the broiler to make sure salmon doesn't scorch in some places, until the sauce sizzles and begins to brown, about 8 minutes for medium doneness, depending on the thickness of the salmon. Serve with Bibb lettuce, rice, and Gochujang Vinaigrette.

VARIATION: Replace the *gochujang* with ½ teaspoon of *gochugaru* and add 1 tablespoon of honey.

SAVORY DUTCH BABY
WITH GOCHUJANG SALMON LEFTOVERS

You might think this is not very Korean, but we think of this baby as a fluffy cousin to all the *jeon* we eat. While we were growing up, *jeon* was a blanket canvas to hide vegetable scraps and meat trimmings. This large, fluffy popover is a great way to showcase leftovers and perfect for an easy but festive brunch. As this bakes, you will be tempted to open the oven door. But resist and do not open the oven door during the 18-minute cooking time, otherwise the baby will deflate. Try replacing the all-purpose flour with sweet rice flour, such as *mochiko*; it won't rise as much, but you will get a *mochi*-like pancake. **MAKES 1 SERVING**

⅓ cup all-purpose flour

½ cup milk (whole milk, skim milk, or half-and-half all work well)

1 large egg

2 teaspoons granulated sugar, or 1 tablespoon pure maple syrup

Pinch of fine sea salt

1 tablespoon unsalted butter, or 1 teaspoon neutral oil, such as canola or grapeseed

OPTIONAL ADD-INS

¼ cup leftover cooked salmon, such as Roasted Salmon with Gochujang Mayo (page 143) + handful of chopped chives

5 to 6 perilla leaves, hand torn + ¼ cup Brie, torn into bite-size pieces

¼ cup sautéed kimchi + ¼ cup grated Cheddar

¼ cup chopped Sesame Spinach Banchan (page 102) + ¼ cup Pecorino Romano

Place a 6- to 8-inch ovenproof or cast-iron skillet in the oven. Preheat the oven to 400°F.

Combine the flour, milk, egg, sugar, and salt in a bowl and whisk to remove any clumps. This should yield about 1 cup of batter. Once the oven reaches 400°F, add the butter or oil to the pan and place it back in the oven for 5 minutes.

Add any of the additional ingredient combinations to the batter; pour the batter into the hot buttered pan, and cook for 18 minutes. *Do not open the oven door*, or else the baby will deflate.

VARIATION: For a sweet Dutch baby, omit the listed topping ingredients and top instead with seasonal berries, favorite jams, Nutella, or powdered sugar.

KOREAN-STYLE POKÉ

Hwe Muchim

We've taken *poké*, a Hawaiian raw fish salad often made with local fresh tuna, and jazzed it up with Korean flavors. Feel free to mix up the herbs; if you don't have an Asian grocery near you, experiment with cilantro, watercress, chives, basil, and any vegetables you have hanging out in your garden or refrigerator. This is so good with salmon, but try with other seafood, such as lightly poached shrimp, oysters, tuna, and a dollop of silky *uni*, sea urchin.

MAKES 2 TO 4 SERVINGS

1 cup sliced cucumber, sliced into ⅛-inch rounds

1 teaspoon fine-grain salt

3 tablespoons Gochujang Vinaigrette (page 18), plus more if desired

1 pound best-quality sashimi-grade salmon or tuna (ahi), cut into ½-inch cubes

1½ cups roughly chopped *minari*, watercress, or red leaf lettuce

1½ cups roughly chopped perilla leaves

½ Asian pear or apple such as Fuji or Honeycrisp, thinly sliced

Juice of 1 lime, plus more if desired (optional)

1 teaspoon sesame oil

GARNISH 1 teaspoon toasted sesame seeds

FOR SERVING rice, wonton chips

Place the cucumber slices in a small bowl and sprinkle with the salt; set aside for 15 minutes. Rinse and squeeze out any excess liquid.

Toss the Gochujang Vinaigrette with the salmon pieces in a bowl; cover and let sit in the refrigerator for up to 30 minutes while prepping the other vegetables.

Chop and slice the *minari*, perilla, pear, and any other vegetables you'd like. Toss with the salmon and salted cucumbers. Taste and add more Gochujang Vinaigrette if you want more spice or add fresh lime juice for a bit of zing. Drizzle with the sesame oil and gently toss again. Garnish with the sesame seeds. Serve with rice or wonton chips.

SASHIMI RICE BOWL

Hwedupbap

You might be familiar with Korea's national dish called *bibimbap*, a mixed rice bowl often topped with vegetables and meat. This version is colorful, healthful, and loaded with the freshest raw fish and crunchy vegetables. The Gochujang Vinaigrette (page 18) kick-starts all the flavors and brings everything together. It's very important to make the rice in advance and let it cool to room temperature, as it's being topped with cold fresh fish and vegetables. **MAKES 1 SERVING**

1 cup cooked sushi rice or Quinoa Rice (page 192), at room temperature

2 cups thinly sliced crunchy vegetables, such as lettuce, onion, or cucumber

¼ pound fresh sashimi-grade fish (such as salmon, tuna, or cooked shrimp), cubed

1 teaspoon sesame oil

2 perilla leaves, thinly sliced, or ¼ cup chopped fresh herbs, such as cilantro, mint, or basil

GARNISH ¼ cup crushed toasted seaweed

FOR SERVING 2 tablespoons Gochujang Vinaigrette (page 18)

Place the rice in an individual serving bowl, then add the sliced vegetables in a single layer; place the sashimi on top of the vegetables. Drizzle with the sesame oil and sprinkle with the perilla leaves or chopped herbs. Garnish with the toasted seaweed. Serve with the Gochujang Vinaigrette.

RICE BOWL
WITH ASSORTED VEGETABLE BANCHAN

Namul Bibimbap

Bibimbap, which translates literally to "mixed rice," is a bowl of rice that can be topped with almost anything. In Korea, when cooking at home, *bibimbap* usually means "let's get rid of all the leftovers." A big rice bowl with leftover *banchan*, a few torn lettuce and perilla leaves, and a heaping dose of Gochujang Vinaigrette (page 18), topped with fried eggs, always makes a healthful and delicious meal. Let your creative juices flow and add everything from leftover Beef Bulgogi Meatballs (page 161) and Sautéed Lotus Root with Ginger (page 96) to fish and even leftover Thanksgiving turkey! **MAKES 2 SERVINGS**

2 cups cooked rice, preferably short- or medium-grain

2 large eggs, cooked sunny-side up

OPTIONAL TOPPINGS Shiitake Mushroom Banchan (page 104), Sesame Spinach Banchan (page 102), Fresh Bean Sprout Banchan (page 100), Zucchini with Salted Shrimp (page 110), Daikon Radish Banchan (page 100)

FOR SERVING Gochujang Vinaigrette (page 18)

Divide the cooked rice evenly between two bowls. Top each with a sunny-side up egg and assorted *banchan* and serve with Gochujang Vinaigrette.

Heat a charcoal or electric grill to about 500°F. Cook the meat for 2 minutes on one side, then turn and cook for another minute or so on the other side, or until charred and crisp around the edges. Cook to your preference, just like bacon; some like it crispy, some like it chewy. We think the best bits are right around the bone, so to truly enjoy this part, crispy is better to ensure that the fat renders out completely.

This is best cooked on a grill but can be panfried, then heated under a broiler (8 to 10 minutes, checking and turning every 2 minutes) to mimic the char from a grill.

Serve with lettuce leaves, perilla leaves, fresh warm tortillas, Ssamjang, and warm cooked rice.

BRAISED SHORT RIBS
WITH CINNAMON AND STAR ANISE

Kalbi Jjim

This is a way to celebrate and elevate the cheaper cuts of meat, such as oxtails and short ribs. To make this rich dish really clean and hearty, we take a few extra steps. We cook the meat first and remove the fat rendered from the meat. Then, we cook the vegetables separately in the braising liquid, and combine everything at the end for final cooking. It might seem tedious but it allows every ingredient to be cooked perfectly and maintain its form.

Along with Panfried Stuffed Vegetables (page 38), the smell of braised short ribs or oxtail gets everyone excited during the holidays. Serve with soft polenta, noodles, steamed rice, Focaccia with Fried Kimchi (page 61), or with grilled bread. **MAKES 4 TO 6 SERVINGS**

3 to 4 pounds meaty short ribs or oxtails

6 cups water

⅓ to ½ cup brown sugar, to taste

½ cup low-sodium soy sauce

1 tablespoon aged soy sauce or fish sauce

6 garlic cloves, peeled and halved

One 2-inch piece fresh ginger, thinly sliced

½ small yellow onion, stuck with 5 whole cloves

3 whole star anise (optional)

1 cinnamon stick (optional)

5 dried jujube dates (optional)

2 medium-size carrots, trimmed, peeled, and cut into 3-inch pieces

1 small daikon radish or 2 small turnips, peeled, trimmed, and cut into 3-inch pieces

10 dried shiitake mushroom caps, soaked in hot water, or fresh shiitake, sliced into quarters

1 tablespoon sesame oil

GARNISHES 1 tablespoon pine nuts, Egg Crepes (page 26), 1 tablespoon chopped fresh parsley or green onion

Combine the short ribs and water in a large pot set over medium-high heat. When the water begins to boil, skim the froth from the surface and discard. Add the brown sugar, soy sauce, aged soy sauce, garlic, ginger, onion, and spices, and jujube, if using. Lower the heat to medium-low and braise, partially covered with a lid, until the meat is fork-tender and just starting to fall off the bone: for short ribs, about 2 hours; for oxtails, 3 to 4 hours.

Remove the onion, ginger pieces, and whole spices, if using. Separate the meat and braising liquid, and chill overnight. Remove the fat from the braising liquid and discard. If you're short on time, set the meat aside and chill the broth in the freezer for 3 hours, then remove the fat.

Bring the braising liquid to a simmer. Add the carrots, daikon, and shiitake and reserved meat; cook on medium heat until the vegetables are tender, about 20 minutes. Transfer the vegetables from the broth to a bowl, set aside. Trim the reserved meat, if desired (e.g., remove the bones, cut in bite-size pieces), and add to the braising liquid. Bring to a boil. Stir in the sesame oil, add the cooked vegetables back to the pot, and cook for another 3 to 5 minutes, until all the ingredients are heated through. Garnish with the pine nuts, sliced Egg Crepes, and chopped fresh parsley or onion, if desired.

LEFTOVER BRAISED
SHORT RIB/OXTAIL DUMPLINGS
Mandu

Who doesn't love a good soup dumpling (*xia long bao*)—tender pockets of dough filled with steaming meaty broth? This recipe came about when there was leftover braised oxtail in the refrigerator that had become completely jellified. Using the leftover braising liquid will give the filling a gelatinous texture that then liquefies when steamed. We recommend using Korean dumpling skins, which are slightly thicker than wonton wrappers and also have more give to allow for easier pinching and sealing. These are best steamed so that the soup will liquefy like a soup dumpling. Panfrying is not recommended for this particular recipe as the hot oil can cause the dumplings and the delicate broth inside to explode. **MAKES ABOUT 45 TO 50 DUMPLINGS**

2 cups leftover meat and any small bits of vegetables, preferably from oxtail or Braised Short Ribs (page 158)

½ cup chilled leftover braising liquid from oxtail or Braised Short Ribs (page 158), chilled and cut into cubes

½ cup chopped chives or green onions

1 cup drained ricotta

50 store-bought dumpling skins

4 to 5 napa cabbage leaves

FOR SERVING Soy-Vinegar Dipping Sauce (page 21)

Using a fork, mash the leftover meat in a bowl along with the vegetables with the leftover chilled braising liquid cubes. Stir in the chives and the ricotta; mix just to combine.

To assemble the *mandu*, place about 2 teaspoons of the filling in the center of each wrapper. Dip your fingertip in a glass of water and paint around the edge of the wrapper. Fold the wrapper over to the center and close at the top and twist (like the wrapper on a Hershey's kiss chocolate candy), or other preferred method of closing a dumpling (see photo, pages 54–56). The dumplings can be frozen at this point: Line a baking sheet or cutting board that fits your freezer with parchment paper, and freeze the *mandu* for at least 1 hour. Once firm to the touch, store in resealable bags in the freezer for up to 2 months.

In a large pot that fits your steamer, bring a few cups of water to a boil over high heat. Line the steamer with napa cabbage leaves. Carefully place the dumplings in the steamer basket in one layer so that the dumplings are not touching. Cover and steam the dumplings for 7 minutes if fresh and 9 to 10 if frozen. Serve with the Soy-Vinegar Dipping Sauce.

BEEF BULGOGI MEATBALLS

Bulgogi, one of Korea's most popular beef dishes made of very thin slices marinated and then grilled at a very hot tableside grill, is often served in restaurants. At home, getting the thin bits of beef crispy is hard to mimic and often results in overcooked and anemic-looking meat, so we took the flavors of *bulgogi* and made mini meatballs for sliders or to top rice bowls. If you want a classic *bulgogi* marinade, go to Beef on a Stick (page 153) for a KBBQ marinade that works on just about any thinly sliced meat. **MAKES 18 SLIDER PATTIES OR 40 TO 50 MINI MEATBALLS**

¼ cup low-sodium soy sauce

2 teaspoons fish sauce

3 tablespoons dark brown sugar

¼ Asian pear, or Bosc or Bartlett pear, grated

2 tablespoons minced garlic

3 tablespoons minced green onion

¾ teaspoon freshly ground black pepper

2 tablespoons toasted sesame oil

1 large egg, lightly beaten

⅓ cup homemade dried bread crumbs or panko

1 pound ground beef, preferably chuck and short rib

1 pound ground pork or veal

Neutral oil, such as canola or grapeseed, for panfrying (optional)

8 small slider buns, such as brioche or sesame buns or lettuce leaves and steamed rice

OPTIONAL TOPPINGS Cheddar, mayonnaise, mustard, Ssamjang (page 20), Soy-Vinegar Dipping Sauce (page 21)

Combine the soy sauce, fish sauce, brown sugar, pear, garlic, green onion, black pepper, and sesame oil in a large bowl; whisk well. Add the egg, bread crumbs, and ground meats and mix just to combine all the ingredients, being careful not to overmix. Cover and let chill in the refrigerator for 30 minutes and up to 2 hours.

Preheat the oven to 425°F. Form the meat mixture into about 18 slider patties or 40 to 50 mini meatballs and place on a baking sheet. Bake the patties or meatballs until golden and cooked through but still tender and moist, 18 to 20 minutes, turning the pan halfway through cooking time to ensure even cooking. Alternatively, heat about 1 tablespoon of neutral oil in a large pan over medium-high heat. Add the patties or meatballs, being careful not to overcrowd the pan. Cook, shaking the pan occasionally, until the meat starts to brown on one side, about 3 minutes. Gently turn and cook for another 3 to 4 minutes, or until the meatballs are just cooked through and still tender.

If making sliders and adding cheese, top the patties with cheese about 2 minutes before the cooking time is over. Toast the slider buns and top with the patties and extra pan sauce and your favorite toppings. Meatballs can be served with lettuce leaves and rice, or on top of rice bowls.

NOTE: Leftover meatballs can be crumbled and used for Morning-After Bulgogi Meatball Poutine (page 164) or on Rice Bowl with Assorted Vegetable Banchan (page 150).

MORNING-AFTER
BULGOGI MEATBALL POUTINE

Poutine, a French Canadian staple in diners and pubs is a "hot mess" of a dish featuring potatoes topped with gravy and curds and is the inspiration for this morning-after cure-all for those who might have indulged in a little too much *soju* (or wine or IPA) the night before. This tastes best made with freshly made French fries, but as a quick remedy, it's great with any leftover potatoes or even frozen tots. We like the addition of leftover Beef Bulgogi Meatballs (page 161) but you could top with just the egg and some extra hot sauce or a drizzle of aged soy sauce. **MAKES 2 SERVINGS**

2 tablespoons neutral oil, such as canola or grapeseed

About 3 cups leftover French fries, leftover cooked potatoes, or frozen tot–style potatoes

3 to 4 leftover Beef Bulgogi Meatballs (page 161) or leftover ham, bacon, roasted chicken, or pulled pork

About 1 cup leftover gravy from Beef Bulgogi Meatballs (page 161)

½ cup cheese curds or grated fresh mozzarella or queso fresco

About 1 tablespoon chopped green onion and thinly sliced jalapeño pepper

OPTIONAL GARNISHES fried egg, aged soy sauce, hot sauce

Place 2 tablespoons of oil in a large skillet and heat over medium-high heat. Add the potatoes and cook until crisp and golden. Transfer to a warm plate. Heat the leftover meatballs and any gravy in the same skillet until warmed through; spoon over the potatoes. Top with the cheese curds, green onion, and jalapeño. Garnish with an egg, aged soy sauce, or hot sauce, if desired. Serve hot.

EMERGENCY
PORK STIR-FRY

This is a quick and easy dish that's a cross between *bulgogi* and a teriyaki stir-fry. The sauce is equal parts soy sauce, oyster sauce, brown sugar, and water. Try with chicken, beef, and/or include other vegetables or mushrooms. Makes a perfect meal for two over rice. **MAKES 2 SERVINGS**

2 tablespoons soy sauce

2 tablespoons oyster sauce

2 tablespoons brown sugar

2 tablespoons water

1 teaspoon toasted sesame oil

1 teaspoon minced fresh ginger

1 teaspoon *gochugaru*

¾ pound pork belly, cut into thick slices, or pork (shoulder, tenderloin) cut into bite-size pieces

Cooking spray

½ white onion, sliced lengthwise

2 green onions, sliced into 1-inch matchsticks

FOR SERVING cooked rice

GARNISHES fried egg, chopped chives, lemon wedges

Combine the soy sauce, oyster sauce, brown sugar, water, sesame oil, ginger, and *gochugaru* in a small bowl; stir well. Add the pork. Use your hands to incorporate the sauce into the meat. Let sit for about 10 minutes. Heat a heavy-bottomed pan or cast-iron skillet. Spray with cooking oil. Pour the meat into the very hot pan. Stirring occasionally (you want the meat to char but not burn), sauté for 1 to 2 minutes and then add the onion and green onions. Continue to cook over high to medium-high heat until the pork is cooked through, 6 to 8 minutes. Serve over a bowl of rice. Garnish with fried egg, chives, and lemon wedges, as desired.

KIMCHI AND PORK STIR-FRY

Kimchi Jeyook Bokkeum

Kimchi and pork are a match made in heaven. This recipe is, without a doubt, a crowd-pleaser, but is also great as a quick weeknight dinner option. We call for green cabbage and onions for the vegetables, but you can include any of your favorites, such as broccoli, peppers, and mushrooms. Also, this dish reheats well.

MAKES 3 TO 4 SERVINGS

2 tablespoons *gochujang*

2 tablespoons *gochugaru*

2 tablespoons mirin

1 tablespoon low-sodium soy sauce

1 tablespoon minced garlic

1 teaspoon minced fresh ginger

1 pound sliced pork belly or pork shoulder, cut into ¼-inch-thick, bite-size pieces

1 tablespoon neutral oil, such as canola or grapeseed, or bacon or duck fat

2 cups kimchi, store-bought or homemade (page 134), chopped about ¼-inch thick

½ yellow or white onion, thinly sliced

OPTIONAL GARNISHES 2 green onions, sliced on the bias; ½ teaspoon toasted sesame seeds

FOR SERVING steamed rice, lettuce or thin cabbage leaves, Ssamjang (page 20)

Combine the *gochujang*, *gochugaru*, mirin, soy sauce, garlic, and ginger in a large bowl. Add the pork belly to the bowl.

Heat the oil in a large wok or skillet and sauté the kimchi and onion until the onion becomes translucent and starts to caramelize, about 5 minutes; remove from the heat and transfer to a plate. Carefully wipe out the wok with a paper towel, then reheat the wok over high heat. Add the pork to the hot wok and cook, stirring occasionally. You want the edges of the meat to char and crisp up. When the pork is almost cooked, after 8 to 10 minutes over medium-high heat, add the kimchi mixture to the pork. Sauté for about 2 minutes. Garnish with the green onions and sesame seeds. Serve hot with steamed rice, lettuce leaves, and *ssamjang*.

STEAMED PORK VEGETABLE WRAPS

Bossam

Ask any Korean about making kimchi and they will tell you the pork dish they make to pair with fresh kimchi is always *bossam*. *Bossam* is typically served with salted napa cabbage and Radish Kimchi with Oysters (page 128). You can also serve this with a dozen fresh shucked oysters on the side. Deconstructed or not, the flavors work well together. Serve with a few slices of garlic, chiles, and a small bowl of salted shrimp; the enzymes in salted shrimp help digest fatty meats, so you can eat more pork. **MAKES 4 SERVINGS**

FOR THE SALTED NAPA CABBAGE LEAVES

4 cups water

¼ cup salt

15 napa cabbage leaves

FOR THE PORK

One 3- to 4-pound pork shoulder or butt or pork belly

1 cup *soju*, sake, or lager (optional)

1 tablespoon *doenjang*

One 2-inch piece fresh ginger

½ yellow or white onion

About 6 black peppercorns, or 1 teaspoon crushed black pepper

1 cinnamon stick

3 whole cloves

2 star anise

2 to 3 black cardamom seeds

2 bay leaves

OPTIONAL GARNISH 1 to 2 tablespoons chopped green onion

FOR SERVING Ssamjang (page 20) or Emergency Ssamjang (page 20), Radish Kimchi with Oysters (page 128), lettuce leaves, perilla leaves, steamed rice, garlic, chiles, and salted shrimp

Make the salted napa cabbage leaves: Combine the water and salt in a large bowl and submerge the cabbage leaves. Place a plate over the top to keep the leaves submerged and let sit about 4 hours. Tip: The stem of the leaf should gently bend backward without snapping. Rinse under cool running water and drain thoroughly. Cut cabbage into 3-by-4-inch rectangular wrappers.

Make the pork: Trim, if desired, any excess fat from the pork and cut the pork into three equal-sized pieces. Place the pork in a large pot. Add enough water (and alcohol, if using), about 4 cups of total liquid, to cover the meat by about 3 inches. Add the *doenjang*, ginger, white onion, and peppercorns. If desired, add the cinnamon stick, cloves, star anise, cardamom seed, and bay leaves. Bring to a low boil. Lower the heat to medium-low and cook, covered, until the meat is almost fork-tender and juices run clear; you don't want the meat totally falling apart but, rather, tender enough to slice into whole pieces. If using pork belly, the cooking time will increase by about 30 minutes.

Remove the meat from the pot and place in a bowl, cover, and let cool about 20 minutes. Reserve the cooking liquid. To serve: Slice the pork and arrange on a serving platter. Serve, if desired, with small cups of the reserved cooking broth that has been skimmed and strained, and top with chopped green onion.

GOCHUJANG-CURED PORK BELLY BBQ

Gochujang Samgyeopsal Gui

Once you taste this, it might become the star of your next summer BBQ. The *gochujang*-based marinade cures the pork belly to taste like bacon jerky. This is particularly excellent with fresh perilla leaves. **MAKES 4 SERVINGS**

3 tablespoons *gochujang*

3 tablespoons *gochugaru*

2 tablespoons mirin

2 tablespoons soy sauce

2 tablespoons brown sugar

½ onion, grated (optional)

1 tablespoon minced garlic

2 teaspoons minced fresh ginger

½ tablespoon oyster sauce or fish sauce, or 1 tablespoon low-sodium soy sauce

2 pounds pork belly, thick-sliced

FOR SERVING perilla leaves, lettuce leaves, Ssamjang (page 20), cooked rice

Mix together the *gochujang*, *gochugaru*, mirin, soy sauce, brown sugar, onion, garlic, and ginger, and oyster sauce in a large, resealable plastic bag. Add the pork belly, allowing the marinade to coat the pork belly slices evenly. Marinate in the refrigerator for at least 1 hour and up to 24.

Heat the broiler to HIGH and line a baking sheet with aluminum foil. Remove the pork belly from the marinade; discard the marinade. Place the pork belly slices on the prepared baking sheet and broil for 5 minutes, turn the pork over, and cook for another 4 to 5 minutes on the other side and until crisp and caramelized. For more flavor, cook on a charcoal grill. Serve with perilla leaves, lettuce leaves, *ssamjang*, and cooked rice.

MEXICAN-KOREAN CHILAQUILES

This mole sauce was brought up in Puebla and went to finishing school in Korea. Both cultures use dried chiles to create pastes and sauces and add depth to many dishes. This mole is perfect with roasted chicken thighs or breasts, tossed with leftover roast beef or pork, or used to coat fresh homemade tortilla chips and topped with a fried egg for a quick breakfast or snack of chilaquiles. This does require quite a gathering of ingredients, but it makes a large enough amount that you can freeze. **MAKES ABOUT 12 CUPS MOLE PASTE**

10 to 12 ounces total dried chiles, a combination of ancho, guajillo, New Mexico, or pasilla chiles, stemmed and partially seeded

2 cups shelled pecans or raw almonds with skin

2 cups pumpkin seeds

⅔ cup toasted sesame seeds

2 tablespoons *gochugaru*

1 medium-size white or yellow onion, peeled and cut in half

4 to 6 garlic cloves, peeled

1 large ripe tomato, cut in half

3 to 4 medium-size tomatillos, husks removed, cut in half

⅓ cup canola oil, or duck or bacon fat

1 stick *canela* (a.k.a. Mexican or Ceylon cinnamon), or 1 teaspoon ground cinnamon

3 tablespoons dried Mexican oregano

10 whole cloves

¼ teaspoon coriander seeds

14 allspice berries

1 tablespoon fine sea salt

One 2-inch piece fresh ginger, peeled and coarsely chopped

¾ cup dark raisins or currants

6 to 8 ounces Mexican chocolate or bittersweet or semisweet chocolate

2 tablespoons packed brown sugar or honey

3 heaping tablespoons *gochujang*

2 stale corn tortillas, torn or cut into 8 pieces (or 1 thick, day-old piece brioche or baguette), 4 to 5 plain animal crackers, or 2 to 3 graham crackers

¼ cup fresh orange juice

About 5 cups chicken broth

FOR THE CHILAQUILES
MAKES 2 SERVINGS

1 teaspoon vegetable oil, or bacon or duck fat

2 cups prepared Mexican-Korean Mole

1 cup chicken broth

Salt or honey, as needed

6 handfuls tortilla chips

2 sunny-side up eggs

OPTIONAL TOPPINGS thinly sliced radish, jalapeño pepper, cabbage, pico de gallo, sour cream, Cotija cheese, or avocado

Preheat the oven to 350°F. Make sure your kitchen is well ventilated before starting. Spread out the chiles and some of the chile seeds on a dry baking sheet. Spread the pecans and pumpkin seeds on a separate dry baking sheet. Place both sheets in the oven and roast the chiles, pecans, and seeds, turning the pans occasionally, about 15 minutes or until toasted and fragrant, being careful not to let burn; remove the pans from the oven, stir in the sesame seeds and 2 tablespoons of the *gochugaru* into the pecans and pumpkin seeds and let both pans cool.

Heat a large griddle or cast-iron skillet over medium heat. Place the onion, garlic, tomato, and tomatillos in the dry pan and let sear or char, turning occasionally with tongs and cooking until the garlic (about 6 minutes) and onion (about 20 minutes) are soft and tomato and tomatillo skins begin to blacken and blister. If the pan is too small for all the ingredients, cook the vegetables in two batches. Transfer the vegetables, as each kind is ready, to a medium-size bowl.

Wipe out the skillet. Heat about 1 tablespoon of the canola oil in the skillet and add the *canela*, oregano, cloves, coriander, and allspice. Fry until fragrant, about 2 minutes, then transfer to a large bowl. Stir in the salt, ginger, raisins, chocolate, brown sugar, and *gochujang*. Add the torn tortillas to the bowl; set aside.

Place all the ingredients prepared up to this point, plus the orange juice and broth, near a high-powered blender. Place some of each ingredient in the blender along with the orange juice. Process until very smooth,

1 to 2 minutes, adding 2 to 3 tablespoons of chicken broth at a time to facilitate the process. Transfer the puree to a large bowl. Repeat with the remaining ingredients, dividing into several batches, as needed, and adding more chicken broth as needed. You should have a thick paste. Make sure to puree each batch until smooth so that all the ingredients, especially the spices, are ground and well blended. If not, you'll have to strain the mixture through a fine-mesh sieve.

At this point, you can divide the mole between glass jars or containers and freeze until ready to use. Store in the refrigerator for 4 to 5 days or in the freezer for up to 6 months. Before using the mole as a sauce, you'll need to thin it out, using chicken stock or broth or water. If using as a filling, such as in a tamale, you'll want it on the thicker side.

Make the chilaquiles: Heat about 1 teaspoon of vegetable oil in a heavy saucepan or Dutch oven over medium-high heat. Add 2 cups of the mole paste, being careful not to splatter the oil. Stir and cook for about 2 minutes. Add up to 1 cup of broth or water. Lower the heat to medium-low, stir, and cover. Cook, stirring frequently, until the sauce mellows and loses its "raw" flavor, about 20 minutes. Taste and add more salt or honey, as needed.

When the mole is hot, add the tortilla chips and toss and stir, using tongs, to combine. You want most of the chips coated with the mole. Have two plates ready. Divide the mole-coated chips between the plates. Top each with a fried egg and other garnishes of your choice.

DUCK BREAST
WITH CREAMY SOY SAUCE

If you have the time, prep the duck breasts by patting them dry and placing on a small sheet pan or wire cooling rack set over a pan or plate. Store, uncovered, in the refrigerator for up to 24 hours. The natural bitterness of endive works well with the slightly rich sauce; you can substitute bok choy, chicory, frisée, or escarole. If you are not partial to sage, replace with fresh bay leaf or your favorite fresh herb as a garnish just before serving. This sauce is also excellent with duck confit; see variation. **MAKES 2 SERVINGS**

Two 6-ounce duck breasts

Salt and freshly ground black pepper

6 sage leaves

¼ cup dry white wine

2 tablespoons low-sodium soy sauce or ½ tablespoon aged soy sauce

¼ cup heavy cream or crème fraîche

2 large Belgian endives, cut lengthwise into quarters, or bok choy or frisée

GARNISHES Pomegranate arils or sliced Asian pear

Pat dry the duck breasts with paper towels. For best results, dry the duck in the refrigerator for 1 day (see headnote).

If desired, score the skin of the duck in a diamond pattern. Place the duck, skin side down, in a cold heavy-bottomed cast-iron skillet or pan. Season with salt and pepper. Place over medium heat. The rendered fat will start sizzling after about 3 minutes. Place the sage leaves on the duck; tilt the pan slightly and spoon the rendered fat over the leaves. The skin will turn golden brown after about 6 more minutes. Using a spoon, remove any excess rendered fat and set aside for another use or discard.

Turn the duck over and cook until the internal temperature reaches 135°F for medium-rare, 1 to 2 more minutes. Let the meat rest, skin side up, on a cutting board for about 10 minutes. Reserve the sage for garnish, if desired.

Leave about 2 tablespoons of the duck fat in the pan. Add the endive and cook, basting with the fat, over medium-high heat for about 2 minutes. Add the white wine to deglaze the pan. Reduce the wine by half. Add the soy sauce and cream. Let the sauce boil and reduce, gently stirring, and basting the endive, for another 1 to 2 minutes. The consistency should be creamy. Taste the sauce and add salt or pepper, as needed.

Slice the duck breast against the grain and serve with the braised endive and the creamy soy sauce. Garnish with the pomegranate arils and crispy sage leaves.

VARIATION: Replace duck breasts with two confit duck legs. Heat a nonstick skillet or grill pan and when hot, add the confit duck legs, skin side down, and let cook without moving, about 8 minutes, until the skin is crispy and golden. Check the heat and modify if the skin is crisping too quickly and/or starting to burn. Turn the duck legs and cook for another 1 to 2 minutes. Remove from the heat and keep warm; make the sauce as above.

SPICY CHICKEN
WITH RICE CAKES AND CABBAGE

Dak Galbi

This is a spicy comfort-food classic from the city of Chuncheon in the northeast region of South Korea. Many college students from Seoul will get on a train and head to the northeast side of the peninsula to watch the sun rise over the East Sea, then head downtown, where a street full of *dak galbi* restaurants all claim to offer an "authentic" version of this dish. Various add-ins include cooked sweet potato noodles, potatoes, and rice cakes.

Rice cakes (*ddeok*) come in cylindrical shapes but vary in thickness. The thicker ones are often sliced and cooked in soups such as New Year's Day Soup (page 87). Thinner cylinders are commonly found in street foods, such as Braised Rice Cakes (page 69), which are simmered in *gochujang* sauce; the chewy texture and ability to absorb all the flavors make this a much-beloved dish in Korea. We wanted to keep the chicken the star, but feel free to up the amount of rice cakes to 2 cups if you find them as addictive as we do.

The surprise ingredient is a few pinches of hot Madras curry powder added to the spicy marinade. It adds rich depth to the dish and renders it extremely addictive. **MAKES 4 TO 6 SERVINGS**

3 tablespoons *gochujang*

2 to 3 tablespoons *gochugaru*

2 tablespoons low-sodium soy sauce

2 tablespoons granulated sugar

2 tablespoons minced garlic (about 3 large cloves)

1 teaspoon minced fresh ginger

½ teaspoon hot Madras curry powder

½ apple, such as Fuji or Braeburn (no need to peel), grated (optional)

¾ cup chicken broth, preferably homemade

About 2 pounds boneless, skinless chicken thighs (preferably organic), cut into bite-size pieces

1 cup (8 ounces) Korean rice cake (cylinder shape)

1 tablespoon vegetable oil

½ head green or white cabbage, cut into large cubes

1 large carrot, sliced

1 large Yukon gold or other waxy potato or Korean sweet potato, sliced to a similar thickness as the rice cake

FOR SERVING steamed rice and cold beer

Make a marinade by combining the *gochujang*, *gochugaru*, soy sauce, sugar, garlic, ginger, curry powder, and apple, if using, in a large glass or nonreactive metal bowl. Add ¼ cup of the chicken broth to the marinade; stir to combine. Add the chicken pieces. Let sit in the refrigerator for 30 to 60 minutes.

While the chicken is marinating, soak the rice cakes in water, 30 to 60 minutes. Bring a 1-quart pot of water to a boil. Boil the rice cakes for 2 minutes; drain and set aside.

Coat a 12-inch pan or skillet with the vegetable oil and place over medium-high heat. When hot, carefully add the chicken along with the marinade. After you hear a good sizzle for about 30 seconds, add the cabbage, carrots, potato, and the rice cakes. Stir well to coat the vegetables and rice cakes with the sauce. If the chicken starts to stick to the bottom of the pan,

add the remaining ½ cup of chicken broth a few tablespoons at a time. Keep stirring to prevent sticking and burning.

Test the potato slices by piercing with a fork; they should be tender. The dish is ready to eat when the potatoes and chicken are fully cooked, about 30 minutes. Taste and add more broth as needed. Serve with steamed rice and lots of cold beer.

NOTE: Any leftovers make for an excellent fried rice. It's so good that most Koreans will purposefully leave some to make fried rice for a complete meal; *bap*, the Korean word for rice, also signifies "meal." Place about 1 cup of *dak galbi* leftovers in a pan with 2 cups of cooked rice and sauté, mixing well. Serve garnished with dried seaweed, sesame oil, and a fried egg.

GARLIC SOY FRIED CHICKEN

Korean fried chicken, also known as the original KFC, is nice and crispy with a very light batter. The secret is to double fry the chicken. Make sure to cook down the garlic soy glaze until nice and syrupy before brushing onto the chicken; the glaze will appear runny when hot but once it cools, will become thick and glossy. For a salty-sweet combination, add honey or sugar to the sauce. **MAKES 4 TO 6 SERVINGS**

2 pounds chicken wings, tips trimmed and wings split at the joints, if desired

½ cup cornstarch

1 teaspoon garlic powder

½ teaspoon freshly ground black pepper

4 cups vegetable oil, for frying

FOR THE GARLIC-SOY SAUCE

¼ cup minced garlic

½ cup low-sodium soy sauce

¼ cup kelp broth (see variation, page 77), chicken broth, or vegetable broth

3 tablespoons oyster sauce

1 tablespoon vinegar, preferably white or cider

2 tablespoons honey or granulated sugar (optional)

Pat the wings dry. Combine the cornstarch, garlic powder, and pepper in a large resealable plastic bag. Add the wings, seal the bag, and shake to coat.

Pour the oil into a large, heavy-bottomed pot or deep fryer, so that the oil is at least 4 inches deep. Heat the oil to 350°F. Alternatively, you can shallow fry in a large cast-iron skillet in about 1 inch of oil. To test the heat of the oil, add a pinch of flour or a small piece of bread—it should sizzle and dance.

Shake any excess cornstarch from the wings and gently add to the hot oil, 8 to 9 wings at a time, being careful not to overcrowd the pan. Fry, turning once or twice, until the skin is crisp and golden, about 6 minutes. Transfer the fried wings to a paper towel–lined wire cooling rack set over a sheet pan, to drain any excess oil. Maintain the oil temperature at 350°F and fry the next batch. Repeat with the remaining chicken, draining on paper towels after each batch.

Meanwhile, make the sauce: Combine the garlic, soy sauce, broth, oyster sauce, and vinegar and honey, if using, in a medium-size pot. Bring to a boil, then lower heat to a simmer. Cook, stirring occasionally, to reduce the sauce by half, 12 to 15 minutes. Remove from the heat and set aside.

Once all the chicken wings have been fried, remove and discard the paper towels. Place the cooling rack back over the sheet pan. Fry the wings (in the order that they were fried) again at 350°F for 2 to 3 minutes per batch, transferring the double-fried wings to the cooling rack. While the chicken is still hot, brush lightly with the sauce. Serve at once.

EXTRA-CRISPY BAKED CHICKEN WINGS TWO WAYS

So many recipes for "baked" fried wings actually require partial frying. These are truly baked but come out of the oven supercrisp and highly addictive. We like to serve half of the wings with the Sweet and Spicy Wing Sauce and drizzle the other half with warm honey and sesame seeds. Make sure to have plenty of napkins on hand. Once you try these, it's likely they will become your go-to wings for everything from stand-and-snack parties to game nights. Also, you might want to double the sauce recipe; it's great in place of ketchup for a kicked-up burger, stirred into your favorite BBQ sauce, smeared on a piece of bread when making grilled cheese, or as a dipping sauce for sweet potato fries. **MAKES 10 SERVINGS**

FOR THE CHICKEN

About 4½ pounds chicken wings, tips discarded, and cut at the joints, into flats and drumettes, if desired

4 teaspoons baking powder

1 teaspoon onion or garlic powder (optional)

1 teaspoon salt

½ teaspoon freshly ground black pepper

Canola oil to grease foil (optional)

GARNISHES honey; 1 rosemary sprig, if desired; and toasted sesame seeds

FOR THE SWEET AND SPICY WING SAUCE

4 tablespoons ketchup

3 tablespoons *gochugaru*

2 to 3 tablespoons *gochujang*

2 tablespoons low-sodium soy sauce

1 tablespoon rice vinegar or cider vinegar, plus more if needed

1 to 2 tablespoons rice syrup, light corn syrup, or pure maple syrup

1 tablespoon honey or brown sugar, plus more if needed

1 tablespoon apricot or peach preserves, rice syrup, corn syrup, or maple syrup

About ¼ cup water

2 tablespoons minced garlic

Juice from ½ orange, plus one 1-inch strip of zest

Place the chicken in a large colander. Rinse under cold water and pat dry. Place the wings on two wire cooling racks set over two baking sheets and let sit at room temperature for 30 minutes or, preferably, overnight, uncovered, in the refrigerator.

Preheat the oven to 275°F. Combine the baking powder, onion or garlic powder, if using, salt, and pepper in a large bowl. Add the dried wings and toss to coat evenly. Line two baking sheets with aluminum foil (lightly greased) or parchment paper (no need to grease) and divide the seasoned wings equally between the two baking sheets.

Place two oven racks on the lowest levels of the oven and bake the chicken for 30 minutes. Switch the baking sheets, increase the temperature to 425°F, and bake for another 20 to 25 minutes, until golden and extra crispy. There's no need to turn the chicken, but turn the pans around and switch them from one rack to another for even cooking.

Make the sauce: Combine the ketchup, *gochugaru*, *gochujang*, soy sauce, vinegar, rice syrup, honey, apricot preserves, water, garlic, juice, and zest in a medium-size saucepan over medium heat; bring to a low boil. Lower the heat to medium-low and let simmer, stirring occasionally, for about 10 minutes. Taste and add more vinegar or honey, as desired.

When the wings are finished, place half the wings in a large bowl and toss with the sauce; place the sauced wings on one side of a large serving platter. Place the remaining half of (unsauced) wings on the other side of the platter. Lightly warm the honey in a small saucepan, immersing the rosemary sprig in the honey, if using. Drizzle over the unsauced side of the wings and sprinkle with toasted sesame seeds.

FRIED CHICKEN LIVER PO'BOY
WITH MINT AND ASIAN PEAR

Koreans believe in nose-to-tail eating with no waste, so we love to fry up chicken livers for a makeshift po'boy. You can also make this using flavorful chicken thighs or a combination of chicken and livers. As for bread, New Orleans French bread has a crust that's relatively thin but crunchy with a light and airy center. Vietnamese bakeries often carry bread that's similar. **MAKES 4 SERVINGS**

1 pound chicken livers or boneless, skinless chicken thighs

Milk or buttermilk, for soaking

½ cup mayonnaise

1 tablespoon *gochujang* or sriracha

Leaves from 1 bunch mint

¼ Asian pear, finely diced or cut into julienne

½ small red onion, cut in half and thinly sliced

1 lemon, cut into four wedges

¼ cup fine yellow cornmeal

½ cup cornstarch

Neutral oil, such as canola or grapeseed, for frying

Salt

Four 4-inch pieces French bread or other similar bread

FOR SERVING thinly sliced lettuce or perilla leaves, tomato slices, pickled jalapeño pepper, hot sauce

Trim the livers of any excess fat or connective tissue. Soak the livers in a bowl of buttermilk or milk, to cover, in the refrigerator 1 hour and up to 4 hours. Drain the livers through a fine-mesh sieve. If using chicken thighs, trim of any excess fat (no need to soak) and proceed with the recipe as follows.

Stir together the mayonnaise and the *gochujang* in a bowl; set aside. Tear the mint and place in a separate bowl. Add the pear and onion to the mint and squeeze the juice of two of the lemon wedges over the pear mixture, reserving the other two lemon wedges for serving. Set the pear mixture aside.

Combine the cornmeal and cornstarch and a pinch of salt in a resealable plastic bag or a large bowl. Add the livers to the bag and shake to coat evenly or dredge in the bowl of mixture to coat all sides of the livers.

Pour about 1 inch of oil in a large, heavy-bottomed skillet until it reaches 350°F on a deep-fry or instant thermometer. The oil is ready when it starts to shimmer but not smoke. Fry the livers for 3 to 4 minutes per side, turning occasionally. If the livers start to brown too quickly, lower the heat slightly. Drain the fried livers on paper towels and season lightly with salt.

Cut horizontally and lightly toast the bread, if desired. Slather the cut side of each bottom portion of bread with the mayonnaise mixture and pile the livers on top. Top with the pear mixture. Dress, if desired, with lettuce and tomato. Top with the remaining bread halves. Serve with the remaining lemon wedges and hot sauce.

Chapter 7

Carbo-Charged
Rice, Noodles, and Porridge

Rice is more than a staple in Korean cuisine, both for rice bowls as in the national dish of *bibimbap* and porridges; rice is also made into cakes and cylinder shapes for both sweet and savory dishes. *Bap*, which means "cooked rice," is often made using a white short-grain variety. Koreans also eat a lot of noodles made with everything from sweet potato and green tea to buckwheat. As with Italian pasta, the choice of noodle is important to each recipe, which we've indicated throughout.

KIMCHI FRIED RICE

This is the ultimate in Korean comfort food. Store-bought kimchi works just as well as homemade Traditional Napa Cabbage Kimchi (page 134), and this is a great way to finish up any that's starting to get just a little too funky.

The twice-cooked kimchi method is really an important step—we sauté the squeezed kimchi to release excess moisture and then add the kimchi juice back into the fried kimchi, which intensifies the flavor. If you fry wet kimchi, it will steam and you won't get the nice caramelized bits. Also, the *gochugaru* in the kimchi juice can burn, which can then render the dish bitter.

This fried rice is great as is or dressed up with a variety of add-ins and toppings, such as ham or canned (drained) tuna fish. You can be fancy and try adding ground Kobe beef or leftover *bulgogi* or top with salmon roe. We also like including some fresh corn kernels; the tangy kimchi flavor marries well with sweet corn. Our favorite is a simple, beautiful sunny-side up egg; the bright yellow yolk brings everything together. Also, avocado slices add a layer of creaminess that helps to mellow out the kimchi. **MAKES 2 SERVINGS AS A MAIN OR 6 AS A SIDE DISH**

Cooking spray (optional)

1 tablespoon neutral oil, such as canola or grapeseed

2 tablespoons unsalted butter

1½ cups kimchi (store-bought is fine; aged is good, too, if available), chopped and squeezed of any liquid, reserving ¼ cup of the juice

2½ cups leftover cooked rice (at least 1 day old)

OPTIONAL ADDITIONS shredded chicken or ground beef, ½ cup chopped bacon, 1 cup fresh corn

OPTIONAL GARNISHES egg (fried or *sous vide*), green onions, perilla leaves, mozzarella, avocado slices

If adding meat or bacon, spray cooking oil on a large, nonstick pan set over medium-high heat; add the meat and sauté for 1 to 2 minutes, until the meat is slightly browned but not completely cooked or until the bacon renders most of its fat. Remove from the pan and set aside.

Heat the oil and 1 tablespoon of the butter together in a separate nonstick skillet or wok over medium-high heat. Add the squeezed kimchi and sauté; lower the heat to medium and cook, stirring frequently, 7 to 8 minutes. The goal is to slowly brown the kimchi without burning it. Add the cooked meat, if using, and the reserved kimchi juice, and cook until the juice has mostly evaporated, another 2 minutes.

Stir in the corn, if using, and the cooked rice and increase the heat to medium-high. Using a spatula or large spoon, break up any lumps of rice and sauté, tossing and stirring frequently, for 2 minutes. Turn off the heat, add the remaining tablespoon of butter (in pieces), and gently fold until the butter is melted and well incorporated into the rice.

Top, if desired, with a fried egg and green onions or other garnishes. Try sprinkling with a handful of shredded mozzarella and place the pan under the broiler on HIGH for a few minutes for cheesy kimchi fried rice.

KIMCHI FRIED RICE ARANCINI

You might be familiar with these fried rice balls, a Sicilian treat made with leftover risotto and a secret pocket of melted mozzarella in the center. Because we love kimchi fried rice so much and don't want any of it to go to waste, we've made an *Everyday Korean* version. We encourage you to double the kimchi-fried rice recipe just so you can taste these arancini. **MAKES ABOUT 12 ARANCINI**

2 cups packed leftover Kimchi Fried Rice (page 188)

2 cups dried Italian-style bread crumbs or finely ground homemade or panko bread crumbs

3 large eggs, lightly beaten

½ cup grated Parmigiano-Reggiano or Pecorino Romano

½ cup all-purpose flour, for dredging

Pinch of *gochugaru* (optional)

1 to 1½ ounces low-moisture mozzarella, cut into 12 small cubes

Finishing salt, such as Maldon flake or fleur de sel

Vegetable oil, for frying

FOR SERVING Ssamjang (page 20) or Gochujang Sour Cream (page 22)

Chop up any large pieces of kimchi in the leftover kimchi fried rice and place the rice in a bowl. If using panko or homemade bread crumbs, place in a food processor and grind into fine crumbs; add ½ cup to the kimchi rice and pour the remaining 1½ cups of bread crumbs onto a plate.

Add one egg and the Parmigiano-Reggiano to the leftover kimchi fried rice. Stir just to combine. Line a baking sheet with parchment paper; set aside. Beat the remaining two eggs in a shallow bowl and set next to the plate of reserved bread crumbs; season the bread crumbs with a pinch of *gochugaru* and salt, if desired. Sprinkle the flour onto a separate plate. Have the mozzarella cubes ready in a small bowl.

It's important to use dry hands for this next step. Dust your hands with a little flour, scoop up 2 to 3 tablespoons of the kimchi fried mixture and press or gently squeeze the rice together in both hands to form a ball; it's okay if it's not perfect at this point. Slip a cube of the mozzarella into the center of the ball and seal any holes; if needed, dredge again very lightly in the flour and dip the ball in the beaten egg; then roll to coat evenly in the remaining 1½ cups of bread crumbs, pressing and shaping to form a more uniform compact ball. Place on the parchment-lined baking sheet. Continue until all 12 balls are formed and coated.

Deep frying will give you more uniformly shaped arancini. If you prefer this, heat about 4 inches of oil in a deep, wide pot. Alternatively, you can shallow fry by heating ½ inch of oil in a large cast-iron skillet. When the oil is hot (350°F)—drop a bread crumb in the oil and it should bubble right away—gently add the rice balls to the hot oil and cook, over medium-high heat, turning them as needed, for 4 to 5 minutes, until golden brown all over. Using a slotted spoon or spider, lift them one by one, allowing any excess oil to drip; place the fried balls on paper towel–lined plates or a cooling rack. Season with a bit of salt or extra-finely grated Parmigiano-Reggiano as they come out of the fryer. Let cool slightly, about 1 minute, then serve with *ssamjang* or *gochujang* sour cream. Any leftovers can be stored in the refrigerator and reheated in a 350°F oven.

QUINOA RICE

Quinoa-bap

This is a base for many of the main dishes in this book, especially the rice bowl recipes. When serving as a simple, clean main we love adding such aromatics as bay leaf, cinnamon, and cloves.

We usually make this with two parts quinoa, one part short-grain rice, and five parts water. The quick-cooking setting on a rice cooker works well; just slightly reduce the amount of water (see note). **MAKES ABOUT 5 CUPS**

1 cup quinoa

½ cup short-grain rice

2½ cups water

OPTIONAL ADDITIONS 2 or 3 whole garlic cloves, 1 cinnamon stick, 1 to 2 whole star anise, 2 to 3 cardamom pods, 1 fresh bay leaf

Rinse the quinoa and rice in a fine-mesh sieve until the water runs clear. Drain. Place the rinsed quinoa and rice in a medium-size pot set over medium-high heat. Add the water and stir. Add any of the optional additions, if using. When the water boils, lower the heat to a low simmer; look for very small bubbles on the surface. Cover and cook, without stirring, for 20 minutes. Turn off the heat, and, before serving, fluff with a fork, being careful not to smash the rice and quinoa.

NOTE: Alternatively, combine the rinsed quinoa and rice in the bowl of a rice cooker. Add 2¼ cups of water and any of the optional additions, if using. Cook on the quick-cooking setting.

GRANDMA'S SOY SAUCE NOODLES

Ganjang Guksu

This is a simple pantry dish when you might not have many ingredients to work with. Ponzu in place of the soy sauce adds a nice acidity. The classic garnish would be chopped green onions, cucumbers, and hard-boiled egg, but add your personal twist by topping with grilled shrimp or meat, avocado slices, or your favorite garden herbs. **MAKES 2 SERVINGS**

2 tablespoons ponzu sauce, or 1 tablespoon soy sauce + 1 tablespoon fresh lime juice

1 tablespoon granulated sugar

1 tablespoon toasted sesame oil

2 bundles *somen* or green tea noodles cooked, drained, and rinsed per the manufacturer's directions

OPTIONAL TOPPINGS chopped green onion; julienned cucumbers; hard-boiled egg; avocado slices; fresh cilantro, mint, and/or basil

Combine the ponzu, sugar, and sesame oil in a medium-size bowl. Mix well. Toss the cooked noodles with the sauce. Serve in a bowl and garnish with your toppings of choice.

VARIATION: Grandma's Butter Rice.
This is another dish that brings back fond food memories for most Koreans. Add a generous amount of butter and a drizzle of soy sauce to a bowl of freshly cooked warm rice and mix. Serve with toasted seaweed to make a mini seaweed-rice wrap and watch the kids smile.

BAMBOO SHOOT RICE

Juksoonbap

Bamboo shoots, like asparagus, are a welcome sign of spring. You can buy fresh peeled and vacuum-sealed whole bamboo shoots in the refrigerator section of many Asian markets. If you are lucky and find fresh bamboo, select stalks that are heavy and firm, with a smooth outer skin that is shiny and almost leatherlike. Peel away the tough outer skin and discard. Cut off the tough root end. We recommend boiling fresh bamboo in the white water you get when you wash the rice, which helps remove any bitterness naturally found in bamboo. For a more substantial meal, add butternut squash cubes, about ½ cup per 1 cup of rice. **MAKES 4 SERVINGS AS AN ACCOMPANIMENT**

1 bamboo shoot (see headnote)

2 cups rice, preferably short-grain, rinsed (reserve 4 cups of the white rinse water)

2¼ cups water

OPTIONAL ADDITIONS 5 to 6 jujubes; 5 to 6 garlic cloves, peeled; 1 cinnamon stick; 1 whole star anise

FOR SERVING Everyday Korean All-Purpose Sauce (optional, page 25) or various *banchan*

If using fresh, peeled, and poached bamboo shoot, skip to the next paragraph. Otherwise, prepare the raw bamboo shoot. If the skin is on, cut the bamboo shoot in half lengthwise, peel away the tough outer skin, and harvest the tender shoot inside. Place the shoot in a pot with 4 cups of the white water from when you washed the rice. Bring to a boil, then lower the heat and simmer for 30 minutes, until tender. Let cool in the pot. Rinse, using cold water, and set aside.

Place the rice and 2¼ cups of fresh water in a rice cooker or heavy-bottomed pot and let sit for 30 minutes. Slice the bamboo shoots lengthwise, going against the grain. Divide the shoots evenly over the rice. Add the jujubes or other optional ingredients. Cook per the rice cooker instructions, or bring to a boil in the pot, stir, and lower heat to a low simmer, then cover and cook undisturbed for 20 minutes. Turn off the heat and, without removing the lid, let the rice continue to steam another 10 to 15 minutes. Gently fluff the rice with a fork. Drizzle, if desired, with Everyday Korean All-Purpose Sauce. Or serve with various vegetable side dishes (*banchan*) for a cleansing meal.

KIMCHI BACON MAC AND CHEESE

Kimchi, bacon, and Cheddar seem like an unlikely trio, but they all come together beautifully; the trick is to sauté the kimchi in butter to soften the funk. We absolutely adore this dish; the only problem is to figure out how to portion control the kimchi-bacon-mac-and-cheese addicts around our households. **MAKES 4 TO 6 SERVINGS**

4 to 6 slices bacon, diced

1 tablespoon unsalted butter

14 ounces kimchi (store-bought is fine), drained and chopped

3 tablespoons all-purpose flour

2 to 3 cups whole or semi-skim milk

1 pound cooked short pasta, such as elbow macaroni, fusilli, or penne rigate

Freshly ground black pepper

Dash of hot sauce

8 ounces grated Comté or Cheddar, or a combination of both

GARNISH thinly sliced green onion

Cook the bacon over medium-high heat in a large, oven-safe skillet for about 7 minutes, until the bacon is cooked through and starting to crisp. If there's more than 3 tablespoons of rendered fat, omit adding the butter. Otherwise, add the butter. Add the chopped kimchi and sauté, stirring occasionally, for 5 to 8 minutes. Sprinkle the flour over the kimchi, stir, and cook for 1 minute. Add 2 cups of the milk and, stirring constantly, bring to a boil, then lower the heat to medium-low and cook, stirring, until the sauce is slightly thickened. Stir in the cooked pasta, pepper, and hot sauce, if using. Add a little more milk if too thick. Turn off the heat and stir in the cheeses. If the mixture is thick, add a little bit more milk. Taste and adjust seasoning as you add more milk. Garnish with green onion and serve at once.

SWEET POTATO NOODLES
WITH ASSORTED VEGETABLES

Japchae

Jap loosely translates as "hodge-podge," *chae* means "thinly sliced." Literally, this dish is a hodge-podge of thinly sliced everything and very popular in Korea for celebratory and holiday meals. Traditionally, *japchae* was made with more vegetable and less noodle. But as time progressed, *japchae* became more cost-effective to include more noodle.

If you are like us—who feel the more veg the better—you can double the vegetables that we have included here or add other favorites, such as bell pepper, chives, or other mushroom varieties. This recipe looks long and complicated but it can be more streamlined if you prep everything ahead of time that is required for cooking. As you season and cook each vegetable type separately, have four plates on hand—one for each vegetable after cooking. If you are using other vegetables, think the sautéing order from light to dark, mushroom and meat being the last. That way, you just need to simply wipe the pan with paper towel and sauté the next vegetable. And for a meaty version, you can always add thin strips of flank steak (marinate with the mushrooms).

This recipe also calls for thin egg crepes, called *jidan* in Korean, which are optional, but the technique is worth mastering as the eggs are frequently used as a garnish for many recipes (see page 26). Sweet potato noodles, which are gluten-free, offer a lovely toothsome texture full of flavor and color. **MAKES 4 TO 6 SERVINGS**

8 to 10 dried shiitake mushrooms

1 tablespoon plus 2 teaspoons vegetable oil

1½ teaspoons minced garlic

Salt and fresh ground black (or white) pepper

1 cup julienned carrots, blanched, drained, and squeezed dry

1 cup bean sprouts, blanched, drained, and squeezed dry (or thinly sliced sweet onions, no blanching required)

1 cup fresh large spinach leaves (or thinly sliced kale, stems removed and leaves sliced lengthwise), blanched, drained, and squeezed dry, or Chinese chives (no blanching required)

One 8-ounce bag sweet potato noodles (*dang myeon*)

FOR THE JAPCHAE MARINADE FOR MUSHROOMS

1 tablespoon low-sodium soy sauce

2 tablespoons grated Asian pear (optional)

1 teaspoon brown sugar

½ teaspoon minced garlic

½ teaspoon minced green onions

1 teaspoon toasted sesame oil

FOR THE JAPCHAE SAUCE FOR NOODLES

3 tablespoons low-sodium soy sauce

1 tablespoon fish sauce

2 tablespoons brown sugar

1 tablespoon minced garlic

1 tablespoon minced green onion

2 tablespoons toasted sesame oil

2 tablespoons vegetable oil

GARNISHES Egg Crepes (optional, page 26), 1 tablespoon sesame seeds

Soak the mushrooms in hot water to cover (top with a small plate to keep the mushrooms submerged) in a small bowl for at least 30 minutes and up to overnight. Drain and squeeze dry. Slice into thin strips.

Make the mushroom marinade: Combine 1 tablespoon of the soy sauce, grated Asian pear, if using, 1 teaspoon of brown sugar, ½ teaspoon of garlic, ½ teaspoon of green onion, and 1 teaspoon of sesame oil in a medium-size bowl and add the mushroom slices.

Have four large plates ready, one for each vegetable. (For each type of vegetable, except the mushrooms, you'll need ½ teaspoon of vegetable oil, ½ teaspoon of minced garlic, and a pinch of salt and pepper. Double the oil and seasoning if doubling the vegetables.) The goal is to cook the moisture out of each vegetable. Heat a large sauté pan or wok, preferably nonstick for easy cleanup, over medium heat. Add ½ teaspoon of the oil and ½ teaspoon of minced garlic and salt and pepper and start by adding the lighter-colored bean sprouts or onions, and cook, stirring occasionally, for about 1 minute. After the bean sprouts (or onions) are done, spread out on a plate; let cool. In the same pan, add another ½ teaspoon of the vegetable oil and ½ teaspoon of the minced garlic. Cook the carrots; season lightly with salt and pepper. Transfer to a separate plate. Again add ½ teaspoon each of the oil and garlic and salt and pepper and sauté the spinach, transfer to a plate. For the mushrooms, just add ½ teaspoon oil to the pan and sauté the mushrooms with their marinade for a few minutes. Transfer to a plate. You should have four separate plates of seasoned and sautéed vegetables.

Soak the noodles in cool water for 20 minutes; this prevents them from becoming mushy; drain thoroughly. Cook the noodles for 6 to 7 minutes in boiling water or according to the package instructions. When cooking the noodles, add 1 tablespoon of vegetable oil to the water to prevent noodles from becoming mushy and to maintain a nice chewy texture. Drain in a colander and rinse under cool water; set aside.

Make the *japchae* sauce for noodles: Combine 3 tablespoons of the soy sauce, fish sauce, 2 tablespoons of brown sugar, ½ teaspoon of garlic, ½ teaspoon of green onion, and 2 tablespoons of sesame oil in a medium-size bowl; stir well. To preseason and to prevent sticking, add 3 tablespoons of sauce to the noodles.

Heat a large wok over medium heat. Add 1 tablespoon of vegetable oil. Add the cooked noodles and the *japchae* sauce to the wok. Give a quick stir and add all the cooked vegetables. Sauté for about 2 minutes so the noodles will absorb the sauce and flavor. When ready to serve, garnish with the egg crepes and sesame seeds.

NOTE: Can be made to this point 1 to 2 hours ahead. Place in a shallow dish and cover; keep warm in an oven at very low temperature, about 200°F.

BUCKWHEAT NOODLES
AND ASSORTED VEGETABLES WITH GOCHUJANG VINAIGRETTE

Bibimguksu

This rainbow-hued dish is the classic *bibimbap*'s cold noodle sibling, replacing rice with noodles and using crunchy vegetables to create a refreshing cold noodle salad. You can use anything seasonal and fresh; just keep in mind to include a variety of color and texture for maximum wow factor. If using buckwheat or vermicelli rice noodles, cook according to the package directions, then rinse under cold water. It's preferable to use buckwheat noodles, but if using vermicelli, make sure to buy noodles made without potato starch as they will not absorb the sauce as well. **MAKES 4 TO 6 SERVINGS**

FOR THE SPICY SAUCE

¼ cup Gochujang Vinaigrette (page 18)

2 tablespoons honey or preferred sweetener (e.g., pure maple syrup or granulated sugar)

1 tablespoon chopped green onion

1 tablespoon low-sodium soy sauce

1 tablespoon toasted sesame oil

1 tablespoon lightly toasted sesame seeds

FOR THE MILD SAUCE

¼ cup fish sauce

½ cup rice vinegar or cider vinegar

½ cup granulated or brown sugar or preferred sweetener (e.g., pure maple syrup or agave nectar)

Fresh lime juice

2 green onions, chopped

½ cup chopped fresh cilantro, mint, or Thai basil (optional)

FOR THE NOODLES AND VEGETABLES

3 cups cooked buckwheat or green tea noodles (substitution: vermicelli rice noodles without potato starch), rinsed under cold water, drained

1 cup julienned cucumber (English, kirby, or Persian)

1 cup julienned carrot

½ cup julienned red bell pepper

½ cup julienned yellow bell pepper

1 cup radish sprouts or thinly sliced romaine lettuce

1 cup julienned Asian pear or apple, such as Fuji or Brisbane

½ cup shredded cooked chicken or king crab legs or cooked shrimp (optional)

2 soft-boiled eggs, halved (optional)

Make either the spicy or the mild sauce (or both): Combine the ingredients for each sauce in a bowl and mix just until blended.

Arrange the cooked noodles in the center of a large serving dish and place the julienned vegetables, Asian pears, radish sprouts, and roasted chicken or seafood, if using, around the noodles. Alternatively, arrange the noodles, vegetables, and protein in individual bowls big enough for guests to mix on their own. Mix the noodles with the sauce of your choice just before serving. Top the noodles with halved soft-boiled eggs.

SAVORY RICE PORRIDGE

Juk

A version of rice porridge, *juk* in Korean, can be found in many Asian cuisines and despite the various names and forms they are all considered pure comfort food. *Juk* is lauded as restorative, perhaps due to the fact that it's easy on the digestive system—it's often fed to those recovering from surgery or even as a cure for the common cold. Use this recipe as a base and add in your favorite ingredients, such as egg, leftover cooked beef, shrimp, or chicken, and even kimchi; it's also good in place of grits. **MAKES 2 SERVINGS**

1 tablespoon plus ½ teaspoon toasted sesame oil, plus more if needed

1 teaspoon minced garlic

½ cup short-grain rice, such as sushi rice or Arborio

Unsalted butter, if needed (optional)

4 to 5 cups low-sodium chicken broth or vegetable broth

2 cups fresh spinach leaves (optional) or another tender leafy vegetable, such as chard

1 large egg, beaten (optional)

1 teaspoon low-sodium soy sauce

Salt and freshly ground black pepper

OPTIONAL GARNISHES ½ teaspoon toasted sesame seeds and ¼ cup toasted seaweed

Heat 1 tablespoon of the sesame oil in a large soup pot over medium heat. Add the garlic and cook, stirring occasionally, for about 30 seconds. Add the rice and stir to coat the grains with the oil. Cook until every grain is coated with fat (add more oil or a little butter, if needed) and the grains are translucent around the edges but still opaque in the center. Pour in the broth. Cover with a lid, bring to a boil; lower heat to medium-low, and let simmer with the lid slightly ajar, stirring occasionally, for about 20 minutes. At the 15-minute point, if using, add two handfuls of spinach leaves with 5 minutes of cooking time left, or at the 18-minute point, pour the beaten egg, if using, over the *juk*. It should have the consistency of a very wet but creamy risotto. Season with the soy sauce and the remaining ½ teaspoon of sesame oil. Serve in warm bowls and season with the soy sauce, and salt and pepper to taste. Garnish with sesame seeds or toasted seaweed, if desired. To reheat, just add a little bit of water or broth to loosen up the porridge.

VARIATION: QUICK BEEF *JUK*

This is a quick method for making *juk* with leftover rice. The process is similar, but much quicker. **MAKES 2 SERVINGS**

1 tablespoon neutral oil, such as canola or grapeseed

5 ounces ground beef or chicken or pork

1 tablespoon chopped carrot

1 tablespoon chopped onion (optional)

1 tablespoon chopped green bell pepper (optional)

1 teaspoon minced garlic

Salt and freshly ground black pepper

2 cups cooked rice

4 to 5 cups low-sodium chicken broth or vegetable broth

1 teaspoon soy sauce

½ teaspoon toasted sesame oil

OPTIONAL GARNISHES ½ teaspoon toasted sesame seeds and ¼ cup toasted seaweed

Heat the oil in a large soup pot over medium-high heat. Add the beef, carrot, onion, bell pepper, and garlic; cook, stirring occasionally, about 2 minutes. Season with salt and black pepper. Add the cooked rice and pour in the broth. Gently stir to combine the rice with the broth. Cover with a lid and bring to a boil. Simmer, with the lid slightly ajar, stirring occasionally, for about 5 minutes. It should have the consistency of a wet but creamy risotto. Season with soy sauce and sesame oil. Serve in warm bowls, garnished with sesame seeds and toasted seaweed, if desired.

PORK BELLY AND GREEN ONION
ONE-POT RICE

Samgyeopsal Pa Sotbap

This one-pot rice is actually inspired by various rice dishes from around Asia such as sticky rice with Chinese sausage and ginger in a clay pot (*lap cheong fan*), or Japanese seasoned rice with meat cooked in *nabe* (*takikomi gohan*). Here we use pork belly, but this is equally delicious with seafood; try with fish fillets or scallops and add them after the rice has steamed for 10 minutes. **MAKES 2 TO 4 SERVINGS**

FOR THE VEGETABLE BROTH
MAKES 4 CUPS BROTH

5 cups water

4 palm-size kelp sheets

1 to 2 corn cobs (kernels removed and reserved for another use)

2 cups vegetable scraps (carrots peels, green onion bits, onion skin, daikon radish bits)

FOR THE RICE

1 cup short-grain rice

1⅓ cups prepared vegetable broth, chicken broth, or kelp broth (see variation, page 77)

⅓ pound fresh pork belly, sliced, or thick-cut bacon, diced

3 green onions, chopped

Salt and freshly ground black pepper

1 tablespoon low-sodium soy sauce

1 teaspoon toasted sesame oil

1 pinch of chile flakes (optional)

1 large egg yolk (optional)

FOR SERVING Spicy Quick Pickles (page 116)

Make the vegetable broth: Combine all the broth ingredients in a large pot. Simmer for 40 minutes. Strain the liquid into a bowl and discard the solids. You can double or triple the recipe, let cool, and divide into heavy-duty resealable plastic freezer bags to freeze for future use.

Make the rice: Place the rice and 1½ cups of the broth in a heavy-bottomed, lidded pot or Dutch oven. Let soak for 30 minutes. Add the pork belly, cover, and cook until the broth begins to boil. Lower the heat to a low simmer. Cover and cook, without stirring, for 20 minutes. Turn off the heat and let steam for another 10 minutes. Sprinkle with green onions and season with salt and pepper to taste. If desired, increase the heat to high to crisp up the bottom of the rice for about 2 minutes. Just before serving, drizzle with the soy sauce, sesame oil, and chile flakes, if using. Top the rice with an egg yolk, and mix well while the rice is hot. Serve with pickles.

SAVORY
PINE NUT PORRIDGE

Jat Juk

Pine nuts are one of the most luxurious ingredients in Korean cuisine. Here, we make silky and creamy porridge with leftover cold rice. A perfect predinner bite or a light, soothing meal for anyone who needs comfort. You can pulse the rice for a coarser porridge or completely purée for a silky texture. Try replacing half of the water with milk for an even richer version. **MAKES 4 CUPS; ABOUT 2 SERVINGS**

1 cup cooked rice, preferably short-grain, such as Koshihikari or sushi rice

3 to 4 cups water, chicken broth, or vegetable broth

¼ cup pine nuts

Salt

In a blender, combine the rice with 2 cups of the water. Pulse for a coarse texture or puree for a smooth texture. Pour the mixture in a medium-size pot, bring the mixture to a boil over medium-high heat, cook, stirring occasionally, for 3 to 5 minutes, until the mixture thickens like gravy. Meanwhile, pulse the pine nuts with 1 cup of the water to a consistency similar to that of the rice. Pour the mixture into the porridge. Stir well. Cook for another 2 minutes. Add more water to attain your desired consistency. Serve with a side of salt for individual seasoning and spicy *banchan* for a savory experience. The porridge stores well in the refrigerator, in an airtight container, for up to 3 days.

PERILLA LEAF WALNUT PESTO
WITH PASTA

Perilla leaf, a unique fresh herb known as wild sesame, adds a dimension of flavor to classic pesto. We love it with pasta but also with grilled vegetables, fish, chicken, or meat. If you have perilla seed oil, drizzle a bit over the final dish. **MAKES 4 TO 6 SERVINGS**

FOR THE PESTO

MAKES ABOUT 1¼ CUPS

¾ cup tightly packed perilla leaves

½ cup tightly packed fresh basil or flat-leaf parsley leaves (or mint and cilantro)

1 cup whole walnuts, or combination walnuts and pine nuts, lightly toasted

2 to 3 medium-size garlic cloves, peeled and smashed

1 medium-size jalapeño pepper, stemmed (and seeded, if desired) (optional)

½ teaspoon fine sea salt

¼ to ⅓ cup freshly grated Parmigiano-Reggiano or Pecorino Romano

1 tablespoon fresh lemon juice or rice vinegar

About ⅓ cup extra-virgin olive oil, or a combination of grapeseed and perilla seed oil

FOR THE PASTA

1 pound short pasta, such as penne rigate, fusilli, or farfalle

GARNISHES Grated Parmigiano-Reggiano and Gochugaru-Infused Oil (optional, page 80)

Make the pesto: Combine all the pesto ingredients, except the oil, in a food processor and pulse to combine. Slowly drizzle in the oil until well blended. Taste and add more oil or salt, as needed. Alternatively, make this in a mortar and pestle.

Cook the pasta according to the package instructions, reserving 1 cup of the hot pasta water before draining the pasta. Toss the hot pasta with about ½ cup of the pesto. Taste and add some of the pasta water to loosen up the sauce. Add more pesto, salt, or pepper, as desired. Garnish with the cheese and some Gochugaru-Infused Oil, if desired. This is also good chilled as a refreshing pasta salad.

Chapter 8

The Sweet Spot
Desserts

Traditionally, Koreans don't eat a lot of sugar-forward desserts such as cake with thick frosting or fruit pies with ice cream. Meals often conclude with tea and dried fruit of some sort. Many "sweet" options are actually not very sweet at all and mostly focus on the healthful additions such as honey and dried jujube. We've taken some of our favorite "Western" desserts such as the open-faced rustic galette and panna cotta and given them a Korean twist, but you'll also find traditional fried honey cookies and soft rice cakes enjoyed during festivals and other special occasions.

BLACK SESAME PANNA COTTA

We are both in love with panna cotta, a luscious eggless Italian pudding that wins over many fans. This delicate confection can be ruined by being heavy-handed on the gelatin. Unmolding is easy, but keep in mind that you can also serve this right out of the dish.

Black sesame seeds, basically white sesame seeds with their hulls intact, impart a subtle nuttier and smokier flavor than the white seeds. It's important to toast the seeds to coax out even more nuttiness; this also gives the panna cotta a smoky color, so we like to garnish with more seeds and something bright, such as sugared currants or cranberries, slices of pear or kiwi, or a swirl of passion fruit coulis. **MAKES 8 SERVINGS**

Butter or canola or olive oil spray, for greasing

1 cup whole milk

2 teaspoons powdered gelatin

¼ cup black sesame seeds, plus more for garnish

2½ cups heavy cream

½ cup granulated sugar

½ vanilla bean (optional)

Prepare eight ½-cup ramekins or ten 4-ounce mason jars or other glasses by lightly greasing with softened butter or spraying with canola or olive oil spray; wipe out the excess butter or oil gently with a paper towel.

Pour ½ cup of the milk into a bowl and sprinkle the gelatin over it. Let dissolve for 10 to 15 minutes. Meanwhile, in a dry pan, toast the sesame seeds over medium heat for about 8 minutes. Shake the pan occasionally. You might see some smoke or steam depending on the wetness of the seeds, which is fine, but just make sure that the seeds don't burn. When the seeds make popping noises, turn off the heat. Let cool in the pan.

Combine the cream, sugar, and the remaining ½ cup of milk in a saucepan. If using, split the vanilla bean in half lengthwise and scrape the seeds into the saucepan.

Crush the toasted sesame seeds, using mortar and pestle or a clean coffee grinder, to create a loose paste.

Bring the milk mixture to a medium simmer and stir until the sugar dissolves, about 1 minute. Remove the pan from the heat and add the crushed sesame seeds. Let steep for about 10 minutes. Bring the mixture back to a simmer and stir in the gelatin mixture until dissolved, about 1 minute. Strain the mixture through a fine-mesh sieve into a large glass measuring cup with spout (discard the solids). Divide evenly among the prepared ramekins. Let cool and then chill in the refrigerator for at least 6 hours and up to 2 days ahead. Serve straight out of the ramekins or unmold. To unmold, run a sharp knife around the edge of each ramekin, place a serving plate over it, and turn over to gently unmold. If needed, dip the bottom of the ramekin in warm water to help release the panna cotta.

POACHED ASIAN PEARS
WITH BLACK PEPPERCORNS

Baejuk

This is a royal court cuisine recipe known to soothe sore throats. Aside from any healing properties, it's a wonderfully refreshing dessert. The syrup gets a kick from ginger and black peppercorns and works well drizzled over vanilla ice cream or stirred into sparkling water or prosecco. **MAKES 4 SERVINGS**

Two 4-inch pieces fresh ginger, peeled and sliced

5 cups water

2 medium-size Asian pears, peeled and cored

2 tablespoons honey

36 black peppercorns

Granulated sugar

Place the ginger and water in a medium-size pot. Bring to a boil over high heat. Once the water begins to boil, lower the heat to a gentle simmer and cook for 15 minutes.

Meanwhile, slice each Asian pear into six equal pieces. Stud each piece with three peppercorns, about 1-inch apart.

Discard the ginger slices from the water and season the water with the honey; stir to dissolve. Add the pear slices. Bring to a boil, then lower the heat to a low simmer and cook 40 to 50 minutes, until the pears become tender and slightly translucent. Remove from the heat. Can be consumed warm but is best served chilled. Serve cold with the broth and three pear slices per person. Avoid eating the peppercorns.

VARIATION: Reserve the syrup from the poached pears. Place 1 tablespoon of the syrup in a flute glass and top off with prosecco to make a pear sparkler.

FRIED HONEY COOKIES
WITH CINNAMON GINGER SYRUP

Yakgwa

Yakgwa, a Korean cousin to baklava, although more similar to Italian *struffoli* or the sweet South Asian treat known as *gulab jamun*, translates to "medicinal confectionary," mainly due to the honey, which is used for a variety of treatments in traditional Korean medicine. It's also essential in this recipe. We also have made this using maple syrup, which works well but yields a lighter cookie, whereas honey creates a denser version. You can jazz up the syrup by adding other spices, such as star anise, clove, or cardamom. Just so you know, the aroma when you make this cookie is incredibly tempting, but you must let these cool once out of the very hot syrup before popping them in your mouth. Give the cookies some time to cool and you will be rewarded with a nice crunch on the outside and a gooey, flaky center.

After making the cookies, any leftover scraps of dough can be rolled out to about ¼-inch thickness and fried for a crispy treat. **MAKES 24 COOKIES**

FOR THE COOKIES

2 cups all-purpose flour, plus more for dusting

1 teaspoon ground cinnamon

½ teaspoon fine sea salt

¼ cup honey or pure maple syrup

2 tablespoons fresh ginger juice (from two 4-inch pieces of ginger, finely grated and squeezed, see note)

2 teaspoons toasted sesame oil

2 cups plus 2 tablespoons vegetable oil

¼ cup water

24 pine nuts, or 1 to 2 tablespoons toasted white and black sesame seeds (optional)

FOR THE SYRUP

½ cup honey or pure maple syrup

½ cup water

½ cup granulated sugar

One 3-inch cinnamon stick or 1 teaspoon ground cinnamon

One 2-inch piece fresh ginger, sliced into rounds

OPTIONAL SPICES star anise, cloves, cardamom

Make the cookie dough: Place the flour, 1 teaspoon cinnamon, and salt in a food processor and process for 10 seconds to combine. Add the ¼ cup honey, ginger juice, sesame oil, 2 tablespoons of the vegetable oil, and 2 tablespoons of the water and pulse until the dough is crumbly. Add more water, by the tablespoon, and pulse just until the dough comes together. Depending on the humidity level, the amount of water needed will vary. Remove the dough and form a ball; knead on a clean, lightly floured surface for 5 minutes, wrap in plastic wrap, and let rest on the kitchen counter for 10 to 15 minutes.

Split the dough in half. The dough will feel a bit wet. Lightly flour the surface of a large cutting board and roll each piece of dough to a 9-by-4-inch rectangle that's ½ inch thick. Using a cookie cutter that is about 1½-inch diameter (a flower shape is traditional), cut about 12 cookies per rectangle. Poke the center of each cookie with a chopstick. This allows for even cooking and easier placement for the pine nut garnish.

Pour the 2 cups of vegetable oil into a deep, heavy pot. Heat the oil to 330°F. Fry 12 cookies at a time until golden brown on each side, 4 to 5 minutes.

Meanwhile, make the syrup: Combine ½ cup of the honey, water, sugar, cinnamon stick, and ginger slices in a medium-size pot. Add the optional spices now, if using. Bring to a boil, then lower the heat and let simmer, stirring occasionally, for 5 to 10 minutes.

Place a wire cooling rack over parchment paper to catch any syrup drippings. When the cookies are golden brown, take them out of the oil, using a strainer or slotted spoon, and immediately add the cookies to the bubbling syrup. Gently coat the cookies with the syrup and simmer for 1 to 2 minutes. Using the strainer or slotted spoon, remove the cookies from the syrup and let cool on the rack to harden slightly. While warm, stud each cookie with a pine nut in the center or sprinkle with sesame seeds, if using. Enjoy with tea or coffee. If you happen to have any of these left over, they can be stored at room temperature in an airtight container for up to 3 days.

NOTE: Fresh ginger juice is essential in this recipe. Buy a few ginger knobs that are about 6 inches long. Peel about 4 inches. Using a cheese grater or handheld grater placed over a bowl, grate about 4 inches. The extra length helps you grate the amount you need without grating your fingers. Use hands to squeeze the liquid from the grated ginger until only the ginger pulp is left. Alternatively, you can use a juicer.

CANDIED SWEET POTATO BITES

Goguma Mattang

This is a childhood favorite, but still grown-up and sophisticated. The caramel coating is like the outside of a candied apple, while the potatoes remain soft and tender on the inside. Some recipes call for water in the sauce, but using oil makes it less sticky when eating with your hands. We like a salty-sweet combo, but urge you to experiment with your favorite baking flavorings, such as vanilla, cinnamon, or nutmeg.

Korean sweet potatoes (white flesh) are starchier than American sweet potatoes (yellow flesh). But based on our recipe testing, American sweet potatoes work just as well. Try with purple sweet potatoes, too.

MAKES 15 TO 20 PIECES, ENOUGH FOR 4 TO 6 PEOPLE TO SHARE AS DESSERT

1½ pounds sweet potatoes, preferably Korean, or other starchy sweet potatoes, such as Okinawan yams, or 3 sweet potatoes 6 inches long and 2 inches in diameter

4 cups plus 2 tablespoons neutral vegetable oil, such as canola or grapeseed

⅓ cup granulated sugar

½ teaspoon fine sea salt or ground cinnamon or nutmeg (see headnote)

GARNISHES sea salt flakes or black or toasted sesame seeds

Wash and peel the sweet potatoes. Slice into bite-size pieces, about ½ inch thick and 2 inches in length. Rinse under cold water and soak in a bowl of cold water to remove any excess starch, about 10 minutes. Drain well and pat dry.

Heat 4 cups of the oil in a wok to 350°F over medium heat. An easy way to test the oil is by adding a small bit of sweet potato to the oil; it should bubble and float almost immediately when the oil is ready. Add the sweet potatoes to the oil in batches, if needed, to avoid overcrowding, by gliding each piece from the edge of the wok. Use tongs or a spider to keep them from sticking together. Fry until golden brown, about 10 minutes.

Line a baking sheet with paper towel. Test a sweet potato by poking one with a chopstick, it should be easy to pierce through. Remove the fried sweet potatoes from the oil with a slotted spoon or spider and place them on the paper towel to drain any excess oil.

Sprinkle the sugar evenly over the bottom of a 10-inch nonstick pan, drizzle with the remaining 2 tablespoons of vegetable oil, and sprinkle with the fine salt. Over medium heat, without stirring, turn the pan so the sugar melts evenly from the edge of the pan, 4 to 5 minutes; lower the heat to low and cook for 2 to 3 minutes, until the sugar is completely melted and turns the color of a light caramel. Add the sweet potatoes to the sugar and gently toss to coat evenly. It's okay if the caramel does not get on all sides of the sweet potato or a few pieces stick together; it's all delicious. Transfer to a parchment-lined plate and sprinkle with sea salt flakes or sesame seeds. Serve at once.

SOFT KOREAN SWEET RICE CAKES

Injeolmi

Koreans love chewy textures, such as *tteok*, rice cakes, which are a common ingredient in both savory and sweet recipes. *Injeolmi* is slightly savory *ddeok* made with glutinous sweet rice (*chapssal*). In the past, making *tteok* was a community event. To achieve the unique silky texture of these *injeolmi*, a man with a wooden hammer usually pounds the cooked sweet rice and, between each hit, the women fold the batter from the edges back toward the center as it spreads out. The rhythm of the wooden hammer hitting the dough and the movement of the women is a perfectly timed culinary dance.

At home, using a bread maker is the best alternative; alternatively, use the dough hook attachment on a stand mixer or go old-school with a mortar and pestle. The classic coating is roasted soybean flour (*konggaru*), but you can substitute ground toasted black sesame seeds or grated angel food cake. **MAKES 24 PIECES**

1 cup sweet/glutinous rice, soaked in 1 cup of water for at least 3 hours and preferably overnight

¼ cup water

2 tablespoons granulated sugar

1 teaspoon fine sea salt

Neutral oil (for handling the sticky dough)

½ cup roasted soybean flour (*konggaru* in Korean, *kinako* in Japanese)

Pour the soaked rice and soaking water into a rice cooker with the ¼ cup of extra water; alternatively, cook in a medium-size pot, bring to a boil and then lower the heat to low, cook for 20 minutes, turn off the heat, and let steam for 10 minutes. While the rice is hot, add the sugar and salt and mix gently, then let cool to room temperature.

For the fastest and painless option, use a bread maker, add the rice and complete a knead cycle, about 20 minutes. Or, using a stand mixer fitted with the dough hook attachment, mix on medium speed (5 or 6) for 2 minutes, occasionally stopping to fold the batter.

Coat a spatula or hands with oil, when touching the dough to test and transport, to prevent a sticky mess. Once the rice is mostly mashed, the batter will feel wetter. Reduce the mixer speed to low (2 to 4) and every 30 seconds, stop to fold the batter. Repeat this process for 5 minutes. Chill the rice batter in the refrigerator for at least 1 hour, for easy handling.

Line a baking sheet with parchment paper. Spread the roasted soybean flour on the paper. Using oiled hands, pull off half of the rice mixture. Gently fold a few times in your hands, shaping it into a rectangular log. Gently roll the rice log in the soybean flour to coat.

Cut the log into 12 pieces, using a pastry cutter or plates (this is an old trick that grandmas use); do not cut with a knife as the batter will stick. Repeat with the rest of the batter. Sprinkle the remaining soybean flour onto the finished product. Cover with plastic wrap and let rest in the refrigerator for half a day, for the best consistency. If the *injeolmi* hardens, roast it on a lightly greased pan for a few minutes or broil for 2 minutes.

VARIATION: To make *chapssal-ddeok*, Korean-style *mochi*, simply divide the rice batter into 12 portions. Form into balls. Dust a plate with 2 tablespoons of cornstarch. Make an indentation in the center of a portion of the rice batter, as if making a dumpling, spoon on about 2 teaspoons red bean paste, and fold up all sides to form a ball. Roll in the cornstarch and set aside. Repeat until all the balls have been formed.

SWEET RICE
WITH DRIED FRUIT AND NUTS

Yaksik

The name *yaksik*, a classic festive sticky rice dessert, comes from *yak*, meaning "honey" or "medicine," and is a treat that parents feel good about feeding their children. Many recipes call for only brown sugar, but we thought it important to keep the tradition that denotes the name, so we also added some honey. Feeling authentic? Boil *daechu* (jujube, or dried red dates) pits to make a sweet fruity broth and use in place of water, another no-waste practice common among Korean cooks; this provides depth and a gentle acidic note. You can prepare the rice in either a pressure cooker or a rice cooker.

Although it is traditionally served with tea, you can eat this like a granola bar, or as a healthy breakfast substitute. Simply cut it up when chilled, wrap pieces individually in plastic wrap. It keeps very well in the freezer for up to 3 weeks, and is best defrosted overnight in the refrigerator. Otherwise, toss one in your bag before you head out and enjoy as a midday snack. **MAKES ABOUT 24 BARS**

DRY INGREDIENTS

2 cups glutinous rice, soaked overnight in water

1 cup pecans (or walnuts, pumpkin seeds, cashews, or peanuts)

12 jujubes, seeded

½ cup fresh, frozen, preroasted, or canned chestnuts, cut into pieces

½ cup raisins or dried cranberries (optional)

GARNISH ½ cup pine nuts

WET INGREDIENTS

2 cups water

1 to 2 tablespoons low-sodium soy sauce

1 tablespoon aged soy sauce or dark soy sauce

¼ cup honey

½ cup brown sugar

1 tablespoon toasted sesame oil (optional, this makes the *yaksik* savory)

1 teaspoon ground cinnamon (optional, this makes the *yaksik* sweeter)

If using a pressure cooker, place all the dry ingredients, except the pine nuts, in the cooker. Combine the wet ingredients in a bowl and stir until the brown sugar is dissolved. Stir the wet ingredients into the dry ingredients. Close the lid securely and cook over medium-high heat until you hear the whistle (10 to 12 minutes), lower the heat to low, then cook for 5 more minutes. Turn off the heat. Carefully release the pressure from the steam vent.

If using a rice cooker, select the SWEET RICE option, or just press the COOK option, depending on your cooker. When the rice is finished cooking, stir to mix the ingredients well. Cover and let sit on the KEEP WARM option for 30 minutes. (Sweet rice cooks differently than regular rice. Some rice cookers only come with one mode. If your cooker doesn't have the KEEP WARM option, stir the ingredients and cover and press COOK again. It will cook for a significantly shorter period of time than the first cooking duration; it just mimics "steaming.") After 30 minutes, open the rice cooker lid and stir the pine nuts into the cooked rice mixture.

Line a 9-by-12-inch baking sheet with plastic wrap. Pour the rice mixture onto the baking sheet, pressing down into an even layer. Let cool on the countertop. Once cooled, cover and chill in the refrigerator at least 2 hours.

Cut into small pieces, using a paring knife or wooden rice spatula. (Tip: It's easier to cut when the *yaksik* is cold.) If desired, using oiled hands, scoop about 2 tablespoons of *yaksik* and create *yaksik* balls. Garnish each with a pine nut. Otherwise, these are best wrapped individually.

Stores well in the freezer for up to 3 weeks; let defrost in the refrigerator overnight for best texture.

NUT AND SEAWEED BRITTLE

This sweet and salty snack was inspired by a traditional Korean confectionery, *gangjeong*, which is a mixture of glutinous rice, honey, and malt that is boiled and then mixed with nuts. This is delicious with salty caramel ice cream or as is with creamy dark beers. We like it with peanuts or pine nuts, but feel free to switch up with sunflower seeds, walnuts, or pecans. **MAKES ABOUT 2 CUPS**

2 sheets nori seaweed

1 cup granulated sugar

½ cup light corn syrup

¼ cup water

¾ cup peanuts or pine nuts

¼ cup black sesame seeds

2 tablespoons unsalted butter

1 teaspoon baking soda

Line a baking sheet with parchment paper; set aside.

Toast the seaweed in a dry pan over low heat flipping to toast both sides; 5 to 10 seconds. The seaweed will turn slightly green as it toasts. Set aside.

Combine the sugar, corn syrup, and water in a medium-size pot; place over medium-high heat, and bring to a boil. Add the pine nuts and black sesame seeds. Continue to cook for about 10 minutes, or until a candy thermometer reaches 300°F. Another way to test is by dropping the sugar liquid into ice water; it's ready when it hardens right away.

Remove the pot from the heat. Quickly add the butter and baking soda; the mixture will bubble. Crush the seaweed with your hands and fold into the candy mixture.

Pour the mixture onto the parchment paper. Using a spatula, gently spread out into a thin layer. Let cool completely. Once cool enough to handle, peel off the parchment paper and flip the brittle. Break into bite-size pieces. Store in an airtight container for up to 5 days.

PERSIMMON WALNUT ROLLS

Gotgamssam

Semidried persimmons, known as *gotgam* in Korean and *hoshigak* in Japanese, are interchangeable here. Two common shapes are the elongated plump and saggy, and the other, round and squat. For this recipe, shape does not matter; both will be delicious. For the elongated shape, cut the persimmon vertically before rolling, and for the squatty shape, make a cross on top of each persimmon and open up before rolling. You can make your own dried persimmon: select soft but not mushy persimmons, peeling the skin while keeping the top, and use kitchen twine to hang them in a well-lit spot (but not in direct sunlight) that's well ventilated, such as an area of your backyard or balcony. Allow them to dry for at least one month. Test them for dryness—they may need longer, depending on where you hang them. **MAKES ABOUT 8 TO 10 SLICES**

2 plump dried persimmons, or 4 to 5 large, plump, soft dried apricots

5 or 6 walnut halves

Cut the persimmons in half, depending on the shape of your persimmon (see headnote), and remove the seeds. Using your fingers or a rolling pin, roll out and trim to form a long rectangular strip, the sticky center side up. (You can place plastic wrap over it for easier rolling. Remove the plastic wrap and discard.) If using the flat squatty persimmons, cut an X halfway into the persimmon and open it up to make a square. Trim off any hard edges.

Place the walnut halves along the length of the persimmon, then roll the persimmon into a log shape to cover the walnuts—it's similar to making a sushi roll. Press down to stick the edges together. You can wrap tightly in plastic wrap at this point and store in the refrigerator. Using a sharp paring knife, slice as you would a sushi roll or a pinwheel. Serve with Whiskey Chai Cocktail (page 236) or afternoon tea, or in a cup of Cinnamon Ginger Tea (page 233) as a garnish.

PEAR AND NUT GALETTE

Galettes are an easy way way to impress guests; they're basically rustic nonfussy open-faced tarts. The beauty is in the imperfectness of it. This is an easy dough to work; adapted from good friend, Sara Foster, a chef and cookbook author based in North Carolina.

The base of this tart is a ground nut paste called frangipane that we usually make with hazelnuts or walnuts or almonds. The paste puffs up in the oven and marries well with the natural juices from whichever fruit you are using, such as apples, pears, and figs.

If making this with Poached Asian Pears (page 212), use the pears the day of poaching, as they tend to discolor.

MAKES ONE 10-INCH GALETTE

FOR THE CRUST

2 cups all-purpose flour, plus more for dusting

3 tablespoons granulated sugar

½ teaspoon fine sea salt

1 cup (2 sticks) cold unsalted butter, cut into pieces (about 16 pieces)

1 large egg yolk

3 to 4 tablespoons ice-cold milk or water

FOR THE FRANGIPANE

1 cup hazelnuts, toasted, loose skins rubbed off (or walnuts or almonds)

½ cup granulated sugar

¼ cup all-purpose flour

6 tablespoons (¾ stick) unsalted butter, at room temperature

2 large eggs

1 teaspoon pure vanilla extract

FOR THE TOPPING

2 pears from Poached Pears with Black Peppercorns (page 212) or 2 ripe but firm Bosc or Comice pears, preferably with stems attached, or apples, such as Granny Smith or Fuji

1 large egg, lightly beaten

Turbinado sugar, for sprinkling

4 tablespoons (½ stick) unsalted butter, cut into 8 pieces

1 tablespoon apricot jam

FOR SERVING fresh whipped cream or ice cream (optional)

Make the crust: Combine 2 cups of the flour, 3 table-spoons of the granulated sugar, and salt in a food processor (or a large bowl, if not using a processor). Add the butter. Pulse a few times (or cut in 1 cup of the butter with a pastry blender or two forks), until the mixture resembles bread crumbs. Whisk together the egg yolk and 3 tablespoons of the cold milk in a small bowl and pour into the flour mixture, pulsing or mixing, until the dough comes together and starts to form a ball. If the dough is still dry, add up to another tablespoon of milk. Press together with lightly floured hands and form into a flat round; wrap in plastic wrap, and chill for at least 20 minutes and up to overnight. The dough can be frozen and thawed just before using.

Make the frangipane: Pulse the hazelnuts and ¼ cup of the sugar together in a food processor until finely ground but not quite a paste. Add the ¼ cup of flour and pulse to combine. Place the 6 tablespoons of butter and remaining ¼ cup of sugar together in a bowl and beat on medium-high speed with an electric mixer until light and fluffy, 3 to 4 minutes. Add the ground nut mixture and mix to combine well. Add the eggs, one at a time, beating well after each addition. Add the vanilla. Can be made two days ahead and stored in an airtight container in the refrigerator; let sit at room temperature about 30 minutes to 1 hour before using; this will make for easier spreading.

Preheat the oven to 375°F.

Assemble the galette: On a lightly floured surface, roll out the dough into a 12-inch circle; it doesn't have to be perfect. Spread evenly with the frangipane, starting in the center of the crust, using a soft spatula or an offset spatula, leaving about a 2-inch border all around. If using poached pears from our recipe, slice the pears into thin slices but be careful not to slice all the way to the top; leave about ½ inch to the top intact. Using the palm of your hand, gently press down on the pear to fan it out. Gently lift and place on one side of the dough. Repeat with the remaining pears and spread out evenly over the frangipane. If using other raw pears or apples, core and peel the fruit. Cut in half, keeping the stem intact, and slice and fan as explained above. Place on top of the frangipane. Fold about 1 inch of the dough around and over the fruit to form a rim. Brush the rim with the beaten egg, sprinkle with the turbinado sugar, and dot 4 tablespoons of the butter evenly over the pears.

Bake for 50 to 60 minutes, or until the crust is golden and the frangipane is puffed up and bubbling. Remove from the oven. Heat the apricot jam with a little water in a small saucepan and stir to combine. Brush the warm, diluted jam over the pears and let cool at least 10 minutes before slicing. Serve warm as is or with fresh whipped cream or ice cream. If making with poached pears with black peppercorn, remove the peppercorns before eating.

Chapter 9.

Hydration and Libation
Teas and Cocktails

Koreans commonly consume tea after a meal, but also between meals. We've included some of our favorite teas that are not often found in the aisles of grocery stores, but can be easily made with common Korean pantry ingredients, such as ginger, cinnamon, and jujube. You'll also find fun drink ideas that pair well with many of the recipes throughout the book as well as with what you might eat on a regular basis.

SATSUMA TEA
Gyul-cha

When Seung Hee first moved to the United States, she was devastated that she could no longer have *gyul*, a sweet Korean citrus fruit with a tender peel, until she found satsumas in Louisiana. You can use tangerine or mandarins as well. The tea itself has a citrus flavor along with a hint of a somewhat unexpected nutty note. **MAKES 12 SERVINGS**

6 organic satsumas or tangerines

Wash the satsumas carefully, using a food-safe brush; pat dry; peel, and place the peels on a clean brown paper bag to dry in the sun (or by a sunny spot near a window) for 5 to 7 days in the winter, flipping once a day. Alternatively, dry the peels in a 200°F oven for 2 to 3 hours, turning every 40 minutes.

Store in an airtight container, such as a resealable plastic bag, at room temperature.

To make the tea: Steep one whole tangerine peel in 24 ounces of boiling water for at least 5 minutes. Season with honey to taste.

JUJUBE TEA
Daechu-cha

Jujube, also called Chinese or red or Korean date, can be consumed fresh out of hand, but Koreans most commonly include the dried shriveled red fruit in teas and broths for savory dishes, such as Braised Short Ribs (page 158) or sweet dishes, such as yaksik (page 222). This tea is known to help alleviate colds and coughing and believed to alleviate stress, among many other uses. Most important, this tea tastes delicious and is naturally sweet and nutty from the jujube. **MAKES 6 TO 8 CUPS**

2 cups dried jujube

Two 2-inch pieces fresh ginger, thinly sliced into coins

10 cups water

Honey

Combine the jujube and ginger with the water in a slow cooker. Simmer on LOW overnight. Strain and discard the solids. Season with honey to taste. Serve hot or cold. Alternatively, combine all the ingredients in a large pot, bring to a boil, then lower the heat to a low simmer and cook for 2 hours. Remove the solids and discard.

CINNAMON GINGER TEA

Sujeonggwa

This refreshing tea that we refer to as Korean chai is often served at Korean restaurants after the meal. This recipe, adapted from the Taste of Korea Research Institute, is spiked with ginger and cinnamon, which aids in digestion; this tea was also traditionally served to lessen the sting of eating raw garlic. Look for cinnamon sticks in Asian or Mexican markets, which is more economical; Korean or Chinese cinnamon sticks are bigger (similar to tree bark) and sweeter than the smaller sticks (mostly Indonesian cinnamon) sold in jars.

Boiling the ginger and cinnamon separately might seem like an unnecessary step but ginger, if cooked too long, can become bitter. Cinnamon, on the other hand, requires double the amount of time than ginger to really coax the sweetness out of the thick bark. So, even though it is another step and another pot to wash, you will be rewarded with naturally sweet and aromatic tea. Serve this tea chilled or warm. One optional garnish that we love is to add slices of dried persimmon, which plump up and turn into a jellylike consistency; it's a treat that everyone looks forward to when drinking *sujeonggwa*. **MAKES ABOUT 2 QUARTS**

Three 4-inch pieces fresh ginger, peeled and thinly sliced

5 large Korean cinnamon sticks

Honey, agave nectar, or pure maple syrup (optional)

1 tablespoon pine nuts

OPTIONAL GARNISHES sliced dried persimmon and pine nuts

Bring 1 quart of water to boil in a medium-size pot set over medium-high heat. Add the ginger slices, lower the heat to medium-low, and let simmer, uncovered, for 15 minutes. Remove from the heat, remove and discard the ginger, and let the liquid cool. While the ginger is simmering, place 2 quarts of water and the cinnamon sticks in a large pot over medium-high heat and bring to a boil, then lower the heat and let simmer for 30 minutes. Remove and discard the cinnamon sticks, and let the liquid cool. Combine the ginger and cinnamon teas in a large container and add your choice of sweetener, to taste, if desired. Serve warm or chilled, and garnish with sliced dried persimmon and a few pine nuts, if desired.

Freeze any leftover tea in ice cube trays for iced tea or Whiskey Chai Cocktails (page 236).

VARIATION: Ginger Cinnamon Sparkler

MAKE SUJEONGGWA SYRUP: Combine 4 cups of water and 4 ounces of roughly chopped fresh ginger in a pot, place over medium-high heat, and let boil for 15 minutes. Remove and discard the ginger, then add 1 large Korean cinnamon stick or four smaller sticks (about 4 inches long) and boil for 30 to 40 minutes. Add 1 cup of granulated sugar and cook until the liquid is reduced by half. Let cool; discard the cinnamon sticks and strain the liquid into a bowl or container.

To make a sparkler, place 1 tablespoon of the syrup in a glass and top off with prosecco or sparkling water.

WATERMELON SOJU
COCKTAIL

Subak Soju

Artificially flavored *soju*, often referred to as cocktail *soju*, actually tastes good and does the trick of leaving one with a massive hangover all on a student's budget. Nostalgic for the reckless days of partying with artificial lemon, pineapple, and cucumber flavors, with watermelon in its own shell being the favorite, we took a naturalist approach and let fresh watermelon do the job of flavoring this dangerously delicious cocktail; feel free to add more simple syrup or fizz it up with club soda. We also like to rim the glass with salt, spiked with *gochugaru* or turbinado sugar. **MAKES 4 SERVINGS**

2 individual watermelons, halved

One 375-ml bottle *soju*

½ cup simple syrup (page 236)

GARNISHES fresh mint leaves, salt, *gochugaru*, or turbinado sugar for rimming the glass (optional)

Scoop out the watermelon flesh from both halves and place in the bowl of a blender. Add the *soju* and simple syrup; blend to just combine. Strain, discarding the pulp, and serve with ice cubes, garnished with mint leaves.

VARIATION: Watermelon Soju Granita.
Freeze the liquid in a plastic or glass freezerproof container for 2 hours. Scrape every 20 minutes with a fork.

WHISKEY CHAI
COCKTAIL

Koreans love iced chai and whiskey, so they're often both on hand and this is a great way to combine the two. You'll want to make both the Korean iced chai and the simple syrup ahead of time. **MAKES 1 COCKTAIL**

FOR THE SIMPLE SYRUP

1 cup granulated sugar (use ¾ cup for a less sweet syrup)

1 cup water

One 2-inch piece fresh ginger or vanilla bean (see note)

FOR THE COCKTAIL

1 ounce whiskey

2 ounces Cinnamon Ginger Tea (page 233)

1 teaspoon simple syrup or flavored syrup, such as ginger or rhubarb or vanilla

GARNISHES lemon rind or Amarena cherry

Make the simple syrup: Combine the sugar and water in a small pot and bring to a low boil. Let simmer for about 3 minutes, or until all the sugar is dissolved and the liquid is no longer cloudy. If using any flavorings, add them now. Let cool.

Make the cocktail: Combine the whiskey, tea, and simple syrup over ice in a shaker. Shake until frothy and serve up in a cocktail glass. Garnish, if desired.

NOTE: The simple syrup can be stored in a glass jar or other airtight container, in the refrigerator for up to 1 month and for about 2 weeks for flavored. Other flavorings can be added, including cinnamon, star anise, dried or fresh chiles, lavender, lemon verbena, rosemary, citrus rind, and so on. Use simple syrup for sweetening drinks, desserts, and other cocktails.

Chapter 10.

Menu Ideas for Everyday Feasts and Simple Celebrations

Here are some of our favorite combinations of recipes for a variety of occasions and celebrations.

Acknowledgments

KIM SUNÉE:

I am forever grateful to Joy Tutela and the David Black Agency who have been with me from crumbs to stars to kimchi.

Editor Ann Treistman, thank you for your enthusiasm and for giving our book a place to call home. To everyone at The Countryman Press and W. W. Norton who brought our book to life, especially Louise Brockett, Aurora Bell, Nick Caruso (thank you for your gorgeous design!), Devorah Backman, Megan Swartz Gellert, Devon Zahn, Jessica Murphy, Iris Bass, Jane Liddle, and Barbara Mortenson.

Leela Cyd, it was kismet from the beginning, thank you for your poetry and light.

Seung Hee, my talented co-author/book baby mama, Champagne aficionado, food lover, and most importantly, a soul sister for life. I look forward to many more happy moments together in the kitchen and on the road.

For their thoughtful recipe testing—we owe you all lots of Champagne and Cognac—Nora Miller, Joe Bieshelt, Scott Woodham, Dan Ahn, Jen and Mark Hunter, Megan Henry, Dominique Cook, and Kaylah Thomas.

For their enthusiastic taste testing, the Berger-Hancocks: Cindy, Rod, Zoë, and Piper; Carrie, Danny, Chase, and Devin; Allison; Katie and Craig Sevigny; Kari, Emilie, and Bobby; Patsy, Paul, Zoey, and Russ; John and Kirby, Kieran, Lorien; Suzy, Steve, Ash, and Ella; Rebecca Palsha; Kate and Danny Consenstein; Kate Vollrath; Jennifer McGovern and family; Anne Wilkas; Sabrina; Ashley; Keri; Mark, Anna, and Levi . . . and all who have a place at Café Sunée.

For getting us started visually, thanks to the talented Ash Adams.

Also a huge thanks to the Keims, Tuckers, and Hoppes; Daniel, Christa, and Lucy Schumacher; Adolfo Garcia; Sara Foster; Frances Mayes; Chad Haynes and Bob Thweatt; Lee Herrick; Charlotte Druckman; and Steve Bergt for reminding me to breathe.

To Neil and Liam for making every day delicious and joyful.

To all the enthusiastic home cooks and readers. And to my fellow Korean adoptees, I hope this brings you a taste of home.

SEUNG HEE LEE:
This book is dedicated to friends and family who have always been supportive of my culinary aspirations and adventures. I thank all of you who have eaten my food—mostly with joy, but also with constructive criticism (looking at you, Nathan).

To my soul sister Sunée, my eating life and the way I look at champagne changed the day I met you. I couldn't have even dreamt of writing a cookbook without you holding my hand every step of the way. What a tasty journey it has been!

To Leela Cyd, I had the most pleasant experience working with you for a five-day photoshoot. I am still in awe of your professionalism and your images are just stunning. Thank you. Korean food never looked so good.

To Joy Tutela, thank you so much for looking out for us at all times—the good and the bad. I felt so fortunate to have your strong guidance throughout this new journey.

To everyone at The Countryman Press who made this book come together. To Ann Treistman, how lucky for us to have you as our editor!

I am grateful for my followers on social media, @Koreanfusion. It was their cheerful comments that gave me confidence and pushed me further to develop user-friendly recipes.

I am especially happy for my ever-growing relationship with wine, my other fermented obsession next to kimchi. Special thanks to ET & JHY, both of whom got me severely hooked on some seriously good wines. All the bottles we shared! And the ones I had to drink to finish this book.

Lastly, for those of you who will be tasting my food through this book, I thank you.

Glossary

ASIAN PEAR/KOREAN PEAR: These large, fragrant pears have a high water content and a crisp, grainy texture. Usually used in salads and for adding sweetness to pastes and marinades; make sure always to peel them before using. If you can't find these pears, use ripe Bosc or Comice for recipes that call for grated pears.

BANCHAN: The Korean table is incomplete without the inclusion of *banchan*, a.k.a. condiments and side dishes. Think: salsa bar in a Mexican restaurant, which can include everything from salsas to pickled vegetables to limes. One common type of *banchan* is *namul*, made with fresh vegetables blanched and sautéed, then lightly seasoned with salt or with one of the *jang* (soy sauce, *gochujang*, or *doenjang*) and sesame oil for aroma. *Jorim*, which means "braised," is another type of *banchan*, usually root vegetables, such as lotus root or potatoes, whereas *namul* are longer, sometimes leafy vegetables, such as sprouts, julienned radish, or leafy greens.

CABBAGE: Napa cabbage, Chinese cabbage, or *baechu* is commonly used for traditional kimchi recipes. For steaming leaves to make rice wraps, try thin leaves of green or purple cabbage or the frilly savoy variety.

CUCUMBER: Korean cucumbers have a light yellow-green hue and are long and thin with a very thin skin. We call for English (long, semiseedless) or Persian cucumbers; you can also use small kirby or pickling cucumbers. If not using these varieties, make sure to peel off any tough outer skin or spikes and remove some of the seeds.

DATES OR JUJUBES: These dried wrinkled-skinned red dates offer sweet and savory notes. Not to be confused with Medjool dates, which are sticky and very sweet. Considered medicinal in Korean medicine as they are thought to warm the body and balance the chi. Often used as a garnish throughout the book; we also include it for braising meats or to make tea.

DOENJANG: This fermented soybean paste has a deeper color and flavor than Japanese miso, which we sometimes call for as a substitute. We use it as a base for soups and dipping sauces, marinades, and so on. Korean soy sauce is a by-product of *doenjang*.

DRIED ANCHOVIES: These come in various sizes. The large variety (usually larger than 4 inches) is used to make stocks and give natural *gamchilmat* (umami) to broths and other dishes. The smaller variety is commonly used in *banchan*, and, candied with honey, they offer a delicious crunch and a main source of calcium in the Korean diet.

DUMPLING WRAPPERS: *Gyoza* or wonton wrappers are thinner than Korean *mandu* wrappers. They are both delicious, but we personally prefer *gyoza* wrappers for panfrying, and Korean *mandu* wrappers for steaming or for the New Year's Day Soup recipe. Also, if you are new to making dumplings, we recommend using Korean *mandu* wrappers because they tend to have more give and some elasticity that allows for easier shaping and sealing.

EGGS: We often suggest the inclusion of eggs soft-boiled or sunny-side up as a garnish. Get the freshest farm eggs possible as they often have a rich flavor and deeply colored yolks.

FISH SAUCE: This is natural MSG, your secret ingredient, your new best friend. Not meant to be consumed as is, so don't be afraid of the pungent aroma; just a small amount goes a long way. Fish sauce offers a savory depth of flavor and complexity to even the simplest of sauces and most people don't even know it's in the dish. For general cooking and eating, we like Fish Boat 40N or Megachef 30N or

IHA. We also use Three Crabs, but note that it does contain sugar.

GARLIC: A fundamental ingredient in Korean cuisine. Along with the people of Italy and China, Koreans consume some of the most garlic per capita. Garlic seasons just about every single savory dish in this book. But note that quality varies. Most Asian grocery stores actually carry Chinese imported garlic, which tends to be on the dry side. Look for garlic at your local farmers' market or grocery outlets, such as Whole Foods Market or Target, which often carry California organic garlic. We strongly advise to never cook with prechopped garlic, especially for kimchi. Prechopped garlic contains preservatives and the aroma is off-putting for uncooked fermented vegetable preparations.

GINGER: One of the three crucial ingredients, along with garlic and green onion, that make up the holy trinity in Korean cooking. Ginger adds heat and bite to both savory and sweet recipes. This rhizome is also believed to aid in digestion and with inflammation and contains a hefty dose of potassium (415 mg) and magnesium (43 mg) per 100 g of ginger.

GOCHUGARU (KOREAN CHILE POWDER): Coarsely ground, sun-dried Korean chiles are fragrant and an essential ingredient in many of these recipes. Coarsely ground powder is best for kimchi and finely ground for soups and *banchan* preparations. It's best not to substitute crushed red chiles, unless noted; it simply doesn't taste or "bloom" the way Korean *gochugaru* does.

GOCHUJANG: A Korean mother sauce fermented with *gochugaru*, malt flour, and rice flour with rice syrup. Fermentation mellows out the initial "burn your mouth" spiciness and creates a robust satisfying spicy depth that is unlike any other flavor in the world.

GREEN ONION: There are several green onion varieties in Korean grocery stores. *Daepa* resembles leeks and is a bigger sibling to green onions commonly found in American grocery stores. It's good for soups and seasoning for various main dishes. However, for green onion pancakes *pajeon*, Koreans use *jjokpa*, a thin and mild variety similar to green onions commonly found in American grocery stores, which you can use or skinny ones available in the spring time at farmers' markets.

JUJUBES: See dates.

KELP (*DASHIMA*): Also known as kombu. If you've ever watched Iron Chef Morimoto curing fresh fish in between sheets of kombu, you might recognize the long dark dried seaweed that contains intense umami flavors, especially salty and sweet. Commonly sold chopped but experiment with whole pieces and break off when needed. It is a key ingredient in making anchovy-kelp broth that serves as the backbone to many Korean dishes.

KIMCHI: When we call for "kimchi" in a recipe like *jeon* or fried rice we are referring to chopped napa cabbage kimchi, *mat-kimchi*, most commonly found in jars at the grocery store; we encourage you to make your own but store-bought is fine. Some Korean grocery stores might carry aged kimchi (*mukeunji*) that's been aged for 2 to 3 years and becomes extra pungent and funky. Just like funky cheeses, you might have a certain threshold, so approach with caution. Aged kimchi is best with heat-applying preparations, such as Kimchi Fried Rice or Kimchi Bacon Mac and Cheese.

KOREAN CHIVES (*BUCHU*): Unlike other chives that are circular and hollow, Korean chives are flat like grass. You can substitute Chinese chives; both Korean and Chinese chives have a more peppery note than the chives you might find in your super-market. You can substitute these chives or use the green parts from green onions.

LOTUS ROOT (*YEUNKEUN*): This potassium-packed tuber is actually not a root but the stem of the lotus flower rooted in the mud under water. This plant can regulate temperature, like warm-blooded animals, hence being recognized as a warming food in traditional Korean medicine, thought to help blood circulation. In Korea, the leaves and petals are used for herbal tea.

MINARI (WATER DROPWORT): Along with perilla and Korean chives, *minari* is another unique herb that is beloved in Korean cuisine. It has a unique green freshness that adds an interesting layer of flavor in soups or kimchi. It can be found in Korean grocery stores, but if you can't find it, don't fret. It's okay to omit. Not to be confused with hemlock, which looks similar to *minari* but is actually toxic.

MUNG BEAN (*NOKDU*): In Korean, mung bean is *nokdu*, which translates to "green beans," due to its green skin. It is consumed in various ways, including jelly, pancakes, and sprouts. In our mung bean pancake recipe, we call for dried, peeled mung beans also sold as moong dal.

NOODLES: We use specific noodles for each recipe; for instance, sweet potato noodles (*dangmyeon*) for *japchae* and buckwheat noodles (*memil guksu*) for *bibim* noodles. Sweet potato noodles can be replaced with clear vermicelli made with mung beans and water. For *bibim* noodles, you can use other Asian dried noodles that can be consumed cooked and chilled, such as rice vermicelli or *mi fun* (Chinese/Taiwanese thin rice noodles).

OYSTER SAUCE: A Chinese condiment that has gained popularity in Korean cuisine due to its "all-in-one" aspect that adds the saltiness of soy sauce, the sweetness of brown sugar, with a viscosity that gives a glazelike texture. Vegetarians can find alternatives labeled as " vegetarian oyster sauce" or "mushroom sauce." Most authentic brands will have MSG as an ingredient. Based on the most reliable science, MSG is not clinically harmful to your health, thus no reason to avoid it. But if you are avoiding MSG, Kikkoman and Lee Kum Kee Green Label make oyster sauce without.

PERILLA: Commonly known as wild sesame leaf or *kenip*. Although these fragrant leaves are sometimes confused with Japanese shiso, perilla leaves are somewhat sturdier and offer a unique taste sensation; those who first taste it often describe the flavor as a combination of fresh mint, licorice, and cilantro. When in a Korean grocery store, look for perilla seeds and perilla seed oil and try in place of sesame seeds and sesame oil. You will be surprised by its "seafoodlike" properties as well as its one-of-a-kind aroma. *Namul* is delicious drizzled with perilla seed oil. If you have a green thumb, try growing your own perilla. They are low-maintance to grow and in fall, you will be rewarded with flowerbuds that are out of this world when lightly battered and deep fried.

RADISH: Korean radish is a variety of white radish with a firm, crunchy texture, and a wasabi-like kick when raw but softens and sweetens when salted. It is best for radish kimchi recipes and *ggakdugi*, cubed radish kimchi that you can make using our Everyday Korean Kimchi Paste (page 133). They are somewhat elongated with a pale green shade halfway down the radish; they are shorter, stouter, and sturdier than the more commonly referred-to daikon radish, which is longer, thinner, and more readily available in grocery stores.

RICE: For most of the recipes, we specify short-grain rice known as *ssal* in Korean, which is similar to Japanese rice, or sushi rice. Some recipes call for sticky/sweet/glutinous rice, which needs to be rinsed and soaked for several hours and preferably overnight before using. For everyday cooked rice as an accompaniment, a fragrant jasmine is a nice alternative. We've added aromatics and other additions, such as quinoa and fresh bamboo shoot, to some of the rice recipes.

RICE CAKES (*DDEOK*): Not to be confused with the round, crunchy popped variety found in American grocery stores, rice cakes for such savory recipes as New Year's Day Soup or *tteobboki* are tubes or disks made of a short-grain rice paste. It's soft and chewy in freshly cooked dishes, but unlike rice cakes made with sweet glutinous rice, will quickly harden and dry out. *Mochi* is a well-known Japanese name for *chapsaltteok*, which is made with sweet glutinous rice, a Korean version of chewy rice cake stuffed with red bean paste.

RICE FLOUR: For our recipes, we use glutinous rice flour commonly sold under the Blue Star Mochiko brand to make a rice flour paste for kimchi and for rice balls for porridge.

ROYAL COURT CUISINE: Similar to the intricacies of French haute cuisine and Japanese *kaiseki*. Many of Korea's modern-day recipes are rooted in the traditions of royal court cuisine, including the very important elements that represent an emphasis on the balance and harmony of flavors. Balance in taste (letting the ingredients shine) and all that surrounds us; as with yin and yang in Chinese culture, Koreans also seek balance. And harmony in the sense that everything (flavors and ingredients) is well integrated. One significant aspect of a royal dish is to have five colors that represent the cardinal directions: yellow for center, red for south, black for north, green for east, and white for west.

SEAWEED: Toasted or roasted and salted seaweed (*gim*), sold in individual plastic containers, has become a popular snack and can be found in such stores as Costco and Trader Joe's, but is often less expensive in Asian supermarkets.

SESAME OIL: If possible, seek out Asian brands of sesame oil, such as Kadoya (Japanese) or Ottogi or Baekseol (Korean). It is important to purchase toasted sesame oil, which we recommend; if the oil is sold in a clear bottle, the color should be more dark brown than a light amber color. Toasted and untoasted are two completely different ingredients. If using untoasted sesame oil, the dish will NOT taste as it did in our test kitchen.

SESAME SEEDS, WHITE AND BLACK: Many Korean dishes are garnished with toasted sesame seeds. Seek out the toasted variety, as nontoasted can be bland.

SALTED SHRIMP (*SAEU-JEOT*): Found in jars in the refrigerated section of Asian markets. Look for Korean salted shrimp, which is sweet and smells of the sea. We use it to season soups, egg custard, kimchi, and *banchan*, and even for stirring into aioli. It's often a great salt substitute in everything from creamy soups to pastas.

SHAOXING WINE: A Chinese cooking wine that is incredibly aromatic and wonderful in stir-fries or to flavor tofu jerky. The best substitution would be dry vermouth.

SOJU: Korea's national spirit. Think: slightly diluted vodka. We recommend drinking *soju* with plenty of food to avoid a hangover.

SOY SAUCE: Many Asian countries use soy sauce in their cuisine and, trust us, they all taste different. Korean soy sauce comes in two types: *weh-ganjang* (Japanese soy) that is used to add color and *guk-ganjang* (by-product of *doenjang*) which contains more salt and is much lighter in color. *Guk-ganjang* is literally "soy sauce for soups"—but sometimes difficult to find unless you go to a Korean grocery store. To minimize the confusion, we tweaked the recipes (e.g., using both soy and fish sauce to season soups) so that you don't need to buy *guk-ganjang*, except to prepare Fresh Soy-Cured Blue Crabs (page 115). We tested most of our recipes using Kikkoman low-sodium soy sauce.

STOCKS/BROTHS: We give recipes for basic broths but store-bought is fine to substitute in most of the recipes that call for broths. But make sure to use broth; many stocks contain celery, an uncommon ingredient in Korean cooking.

TEMPLE CUISINE: In Buddhist temples, cooking and eating is considered spiritual meditation. Monks and nuns in Korean Buddhist temples observe a vegetarian diet that is considered curative and cleansing. The diet emphasizes non-processed foods. They also avoid five vegetables (*osinchae*): garlic, onions, scallions, chives, and leeks, for their strong flavors; some say these flavors can bring "bad spirit to your mouth" and these vegetables are also known to be distracting and to have an arousing effect.

VINEGAR: Most Koreans use rice or cider vinegar in their cooking. Most of our recipes, unless otherwise stated, have been tested using rice vinegar or cider vinegar. Given that all vinegars have varying levels of acidity, we recommend that you taste as you season and adjust accordingly.

Index